The Wild in Us

The Wild in Us

One Woman's Intuitive Journey of Healing, Guided by the Horses

Thirza Voysey

The Wild in Us

ISBN 13 978-1-7776101-0-4

Book design: Drifter Media
Cover photography: IgorZh and StockSnap

For my babies, Patrick,
and the animals who surround us . . .

You all inspire me to be my best self!

Praise for The Wild in Us

"A beautiful memoir written from a place of love, courage, and compassion. Artistic flow radiates from these pages, as Thirza shares her life experiences with humbleness, humility and humour. *The Wild in Us* will inspire you to keep dreaming and sharing your joy to live your best life."

—GINA VILLARES

"We all have 'the Wild' in us. Thirza shares her story that something was missing, her journey to discover what was holding her back, and how she found her 'Wild.' The book, though, is not just about Thirza, it's about all of us."

—PAT MCCUE

"*The Wild in Us* takes you on a journey like no other. Little snippets of time guiding you through Thirza's world through personal growth and the healing she brings to others. Her connection to the earth and the majestic horses in her life takes you alongside her with every word written. Her words are so beautifully and intimately written as if you are living within the pages of her personal journal, accompanying in the movie of her life. You'll find yourself smiling, feeling your spirits are connected as one.

With each story Thirza shares, you are instantly connected to the spirit, discovering the place within yourself where understanding has been hidden away too deep. She has written so eloquently and powerfully about her understanding of the soul of horses and how they have the ability to guide you through finding balance, peace, and cleansing. Her experiences with anxiety, relationships, and choices to be made are a welcomed space to find healing together while embracing these spiritual guides. You'll be laughing, crying, all the while releasing the past, befriending your emotions, and finding your Wild."

—TRACEY DIAMOND

"*The Wild in Us* is as authentic as it comes in the baring of one's heart and soul. Thirza shares with an openness that not only tells her story; she is clearly driven to motivate others.

The Wild in Us is a beautifully written account of personal experiences that bring light to emotions and thoughts shared by many. In a world where anxiety, depression, and fear continue to be a large part of the human experience, this book is one woman's healing journey that holds the wisdom and power to, at the very least, point others in the direction of their light within."

—CLARA MOON SONG

"Thirza writes with an open and vulnerable heart. Through her heartfelt writing, she teaches us how we too can follow our heart and trust in the universe to let life happen for us. I got chills reading about her horses and how their intuition can heal and transform the lives or the humans they interact with. Thirza teaches us how to live in our Wild and how to connect with each of our chakras and the divine. You will find pieces of yourself as you read and reflect on your own truth. Beautiful!"

—MERCEDES

"I've found myself thinking about some of your stories and tips from the horses over the last few days. Your book is living in me now, as it will live in others soon."

—CAROLYN MASSON

Table of Contents

Prologue
The Wild 03
Why horses? 03
The mythic journey 05
Why now? 06

Part 1: Find Your Medicine
Cornered 09
This is my journey 10
Self-hate 13
New awareness 16
Wake-up call 18
Finding truth 20
Coming out of hiding:
embarking on the soul's journey 22
Dancing with my soul 25
Soul craving 29
India 32
Be in harmony with yourself 36
The nervous system 39
Be Raw Chocolate 40
Returning to horses 45
The Medicine Horses 47
Searching for Soulfarm 50
Raven 56
Moving to the farm 61
Fall arrives 63
One year at Soulfarm 66
Piper comes 68
Luna 71
Luna arrives 74
Horse magic 77

Part 2: Feel Your Magic
Magic 81
How the horses walk with us
through the energy centres 84
Being highly sensitive 85
Horses and sensitivity 87
But first . . . a secret! 89
Connection heals 91
Soulfarm 93
The horses point us to our Wild 94
The energetics 95

Part 3: Be Your Wild
1st Energy Centre/**Root Chakra** **100**
Grounding with an anxious horse 109
Trust 111
Fierce presence 114
Raven the queen 118
Suggestions from the horses for balancing
and cleansing the 1st energy centre 119

2nd Energy Centre/**Sacral Chakra** **122**
Emotional congruence 125
Living the slow life 126
You are enough 128
The horses work in the realm
of the Divine Feminine 130
Flow 132
Sexuality and creativity 134
I see into your soul 136
Our emotions are our superpowers 138
Burning through emotion 140
Painting 142
Dancing with horses 143
Suggestions from the horses for balancing
and cleansing the 2nd energy centre 145

3rd Energy Centre/**Solar Plexus** **148**
Experiencing inner power 150
Control 152
Boundaries 154
Responsibility and high expectations 156
Suggestions from the horses for balancing and cleansing the 3rd energy centre 157

4th Energy Centre/**Heart Chakra** **160**
Joy melts the walls around the heart 162
The haunted heart 166
Why are you protecting your heart? 168
Perfectionism closes our hearts 170
Rainbow is the colour of the heart 171
Wellbeing is our natural state 173
Surrender 177
Breathe 180
Suggestions from the horses for balancing and cleansing the 4th energy centre 181

5th Energy Centre/**Throat Chakra** **184**
Shamanic journeying through the wheel 186
Honesty 188
Hiding 191
Integrity 193
Suggestions from the horses for balancing and cleansing the 5th energy centre 198

6th Energy Centre/**Third Eye** **200**
- Dreams are whispers from your soul 202
- Focus 203
- Follow your soul 205
- The leader is the calmest 207
- Horses don't judge 209
- Thought stopping 210
- Mind/Body connection 211
- Happy...with a Wild heart 213
- Dreaming into being 215
- Suggestions from the horses for balancing and cleansing the 6th energy centre 217

7th Energy Centre/**Crown** **220**
- Oneness 222
- Visions 224
- Making peace with death 226
- Messages 230
- Akashic Records 232
- Circle of 13 235
- Suggestions from the horses for balancing and cleansing the 7th energy centre 237

Conclusion 240
Epilogue 241
Acknowledgements 243
About the author 245
References 246

Prologue

I stood at the fence in awe as she sashayed up to the fence. My heart pounded inside my chest and I could barely breathe. She was like a queen standing before me. I could feel the deep recognition of our souls meeting again, here, in these bodies.

I entered the field and she stood right beside the box of brushes. It was time for us to connect through grooming. So I brushed her and felt her strong, pulsing body under my fingers. The power in her was palpable and I couldn't walk away.

I knew at that moment that sharing my life with her was going to change me to the core — and indeed, it has.

The Wild

"Wild"

DEFINITION, OXFORD LANGUAGES:
Living or growing in the natural environment; not domesticated or cultivated.
Slang: Wild also means excellent, special, or unusual.

The Wild within us is our unique signature beingness. We are each here with our own Wildness that we spend our lives uncovering and expressing in the world. The Wild is the space within each of us where spirit meets earth. Clearly expressing this part of ourselves to the world — this is what it means to be Wild.

"The doors to the world of the wild Self are few but precious. If you have a deep scar, that is a door, if you have an old, old story, that is a door. If you love the sky and the water so much you almost cannot bear it, that is a door. If you yearn for a deeper life, a full life, a sane life, that is a door."

—DR. CLARISSA PINKOLA ESTÉS

Why horses?

Horses partner with our mythic selves. They hook us up with our soul selves so that we can feel deeply who we really are at a soul level. Then, horses show us what is in the way of us living from our souls. They mirror our energetic blockages that hang out in our bodies as old stories and belief systems that we have picked up along our paths.

Horses show us where we are not telling the truth of who we are to ourselves and others. They show us where we are living from our ego and not from our heart. They show us where we are feeling unworthy and where we are closing down our feelings. They show us when we are not grounding into trust, where we are not connecting deeply into our own bodies and into the earth. They show us who we are being in the world and how that differs from who we really are. They mirror the truth.

We partner with horses for healing because they naturally and powerfully work on us to balance our energy centres. These are the places within us where old stories, old belief systems, and old traumas get stuck. When these old energies are stuck in our energetic systems, any number of things can happen in our bodies and our lives. Many ancient wisdom traditions teach about the 7 or 8 main chakras (energy centres) and how each one connects us to a different level of consciousness.

Throughout this book, I'll show you how the horses have helped me walk through these levels of consciousness, heal the energies there, and vibrate at a higher plane as a result.

I'll show you how I started out Wild and how I lost this part of me, by walking in the world and absorbing the cultural messages around me. I'll show you how I, like so many of us, lost my connection to the instinctual and intuitive parts of myself until the horses helped me find them again.

I'll show you how healing these energy centres one at a time, clearing out all the old belief systems and energies, can bring us back to our natural Wildness. The horses and I will teach you what it is to be Wild.

For more information about how the horses do healing work with humans, visit our website: **www.soulfarm.ca**

The mythic journey

We are all here on a mythic journey. It is the same for all of us and similar to a modern day adventure of Alice in Wonderland. It is a mythic journey in that we are born knowing who we are, and we shine who we are until about age six, and then we start to forget, so that by the time we are about 11, we are living our lives for others, and molding ourselves to fit everyone else's idea of who we should be. By this time we are usually bending and shoving ourselves into a box that makes everyone around us feel more comfortable.

Then, at around age 40 (or at least, that's when it was for me), we start to look around and think, "Is this what I'm here for? Is there more to this life? Is there more that I'm supposed to be doing here on earth than watching TV, going to a job every day that I don't really enjoy (or maybe even hate), and taking vacations when I can?"

The mythic journey is our journey back to wholeness. We are born whole, we forget that we are whole, and then we find our way back. This has been my journey. For my whole life, the deepest yearning I've had was to feel free.

When I started to realize that I had more power to create my life than I had believed, the whole universe started to open to me. The journey really began when the curtain began to crack just a little, just enough for me to see beyond. When I started to believe in myself and trust my experiences, the messages started to come. The symbols showed up in my life when I started to ask questions like, "Who am I?" and "Why am I here?" and "Why do I feel so much fear?"

The mythic journey is a path not from one place to another physically, but from one place to another in consciousness. It is the path of magic that we step onto when we start to see that there is more to this life, and that maybe, just maybe, we have a higher self, or soul, that is guiding us along the journey.

Why now?

Now is the time for us to work with horses to heal ourselves because we are intuitive, magical beings who have lost our connection to those parts of ourselves. We were born into a world where these magical parts of ourselves weren't accepted and celebrated and we were asked to be small. Many of us obliged until our bodies rebelled. So many of us have experienced anxiety and/or depression which are huge signs from our souls saying, "This is not working for me."

There is a powerful force for a new way. The energies of the earth are calling for a new way, a way for us to live where we are connected to our magic and expressing that through creations out to the world. Now is the time because we are ready to be free.

"If I paint a wild horse, you might not see the horse . . . but surely you will see the wildness!" —PABLO PICASSO

This is the time for us to feel our Wildness, to tap into these deep, yearning, powerful parts of ourselves. Our Wild is our energetic blueprint that is unique to each one of us. There are leaks within each of us created by belief systems we have inherited or stories we decided were ours. When we plug the leaks, our energy becomes clear and our Wildness shines out from within us.

There are stories to our Wildness. There are fires that we must walk through on our human journey. Each one of the fires is a level of consciousness that we may have to walk through multiple times in our lifetime before we clear the old stories and blocks that we picked up our first time through.

Each of these journeys through the fires presents us with a healing opportunity, and when we do finally heal that level of consciousness for ourselves, our Wildness shines brighter and blessed, out to the greater world to heal humanity, the earth, and all its beings. The horses are coming forward to walk with us through these fires and to stand with us while we reconnect with our wholeness. The horses are holding space for us to rise into our sovereignty.

Attention to this work is essential for the deep healing that is being called for at this time. This attention to our Wildness is being called forth, shouted forth, by spirit, mother earth, and by our own souls. Take a moment. Feel deeply within your own soul. You know that you are reading this because you feel the call within your own heart.

Join us . . . on the journey home.

Part 1:
Find Your Medicine

Cornered

I am standing in the corner of the classroom, my face on fire, tears rolling down my cheeks. My heart pounds, and the shame and anger rise like an inferno inside me. I feel out of control. I know I have the Wild in me, but I don't know what to call it. I am eight years old. In grade three. I am writing a poem like all the other kids when the teacher stands over me.

She exclaims, "What is this?" She picks up my paper and looks right through it to the other side. I am at the height of my undiagnosed childhood anxiety disorder. I've been writing over and over and over my letters with my pencil, panicking that if I don't get it perfect, my parents will die. My teacher just sees misbehaviour; she thinks I'm not listening. She makes me stand in the corner, humiliated, while the other kids go out for recess.

I feel the shame burning inside me. The feeling burns so big that I feel out of control, like I might burst into flames standing there. I vow within my young, innocent head to do everything "good" going forward so that I never have to feel this deep, burning sensation ever again.

But the anxiety actually started two years before this.

This is my journey

As a child, I could feel my Wildness rushing in my body like an electric current. It felt like a tornado of love, overwhelming for my little body.

I am six. I remember lying in the dark. I can feel my consciousness expanding outside of my body. I AM the room I am in . . . I am the whole earth . . . I am the solar system . . . I can feel the planets inside my body. I can feel the pulsating of the entire universe moving inside me. I hold all of it inside my six-year-old body. I am the stars . . . and then my power starts to roll through me. It starts at my genitals and runs upward through the front of my body and out the top of my head. I feel power running through me but it's so big and hard to hold in my small body and I can't hold it . . . and I say no to it. It stops and it doesn't return until much later.

This is about the time that the Obsessive-Compulsive Disorder (OCD) started, my behaviour of fixing shoes and other things so that my parents wouldn't die. This is also when the high anxiety started. I was afraid of everything. For the next 25 years, I wouldn't really experience that feeling of coziness and safety that is such an important feeling for us to have. I was certainly loved by my parents immensely, but for some reason, this wasn't enough to make me feel safe, and it was then that I made a decision in my six-year-old brain that it was not okay to be powerful, that I was not okay, that I was not enough.

I was obsessed with the fear that my parents were going to die. I was terrified to be abandoned and to feel pain and loss. This obsession took over my young mind and I started to do things that made me feel like I had some semblance of control, like fixing people's shoes in the entryway of our house, like touching things "just right," and saying good night "just right." It was a lot of pressure for a little girl who has the impulse to be carefree, but who also has this feeling of responsibility for the life of her parents.

I was able to keep my OCD mostly hidden for a few years, but by the time I was eight, it was starting to manifest at school. I would write a word and start to go over and over it to make each letter "perfect." My obsession was connected to the control that I felt when things were done perfectly. I felt like if I could do it perfectly, then everyone would be safe.

When I lost my connection to my power, I started on the perfectionism train in a big way, and I've been on it ever since. Subconsciously, I had decided that if I was perfect enough, I would be loved. My whole growing up, I turned myself inside out to be as perfect and as "good" as possible so that I would be accepted and loved and not abandoned. My biggest fear was that people would disapprove of me and then I would be alone. Even now, writing this, I have a ball of tightness in my solar plexus at the thought of being disapproved of.

The fear of seeing the look of disappointment in my parents' eyes kept me "good" through my teens until, at 16, I was brought home drunk by my friends. I can't even remember the look on my parents' faces.

Constant vigilance about what you are doing or saying because of the fear of stepping out of line and being disapproved of is a long and draining battle against yourself. Many of us have experienced it. Still, at 42, I am experiencing this, and just did this morning. Luckily now, I have enough self-awareness to catch myself falling into the old trap of feeling not good enough, struggling to be accepted and approved of, and dipping deeply into inadequacy.

My brother, two years older than me, was always mad that I was so "perfect." He made comments throughout our childhood that I was "the good girl."

This constant worry continued throughout my childhood with moments of free abandon and childishness thrown in. There were many moments where I would remember who I was and play or sing or dance with abandon, but they were short-lived. I am someone who is naturally boisterous and I like to have fun while singing loud, but if anyone asked me to be quiet, I took it personally and felt it like a shot to the heart.

Self-hate

All I wanted was to be perfect.

My friends from elementary school tell me that at 11, I was counting calories. It was a fad, so I took it on as something I could do. I saw it as another way I could have control. I also was competitive in my self-control, and subconsciously was trying to do a better job than everyone else at it.

Restriction of food is not only unhealthy in a child this age, it is incredibly dangerous. The belly aches started at about age 12. Every night, I would lie on the carpet in pain after I finished eating dinner. I had deep gut pain. This indicator that I was unable to "digest" life as it was, was lost on me.

At 14, I started to restrict my food intake even more. My food intake seemed to be the only thing I could control, and so I did — in a big way. It was "helpful" that someone in my family suggested that I might be lactose intolerant (because of all my gut pain) and removing dairy helped. I say this was "helpful" because it gave me a plausible reason to avoid baked goods without having to explain why. I was anorexic. My body and food were my obsession. But again, I kept it pretty hidden. I have a Scorpio moon; the moon is about the emotions. Scorpios like to have secrets. I became great at keeping my emotions a secret.

Keeping my emotions, fears, and anxieties hidden from the world and those close to me was a huge part of how I had learned to cope in the world. I was in a sea of loneliness, pretending on the outside that all was great and that my life was perfect, while wasting away physically and dying inside.

When I was a teen, my parents tried to help me with my gut issues. They took me to doctors and naturopaths, for surgeries and tests to find a cause for my pain. But they found nothing. They diagnosed me with Irritable Bowel Syndrome, which was definitely the case. I coped by restricting food, while obsessing constantly about what I would eat.

I remember wanting a chocolate bar one day when I was 16. I thought back on what I had eaten that day (a friend and I used to call each other every night and compare what we'd eaten) and decided that if I went for a run, I could eat a chocolate bar. I went out for a long run and ended up at the corner store. I bought one of those dark chocolate truffle bars that melt in your mouth. I remember getting home and sitting in my room with that bar. I remember feelings of pleasure and shame swirling through me. I can still feel these contrasting feelings coursing through me and crashing against each other.

With the first bite of that melty bar, my whole being was melting in pleasure and surrendering to the goodness of this thing, while my guts were as tight as a twisted rubber band. The opposing feelings within me during this experience were so poignant. It was the first time I really noticed that I was "going against myself." I would continue to do it for many more years.

I became really good at being out of alignment with my inner being.

I moved out and went to university at 17. This made it even easier to restrict my food without anybody watching over me. And so I got worse. I was never so dangerously thin that I had to be hospitalized. Somehow, I kept myself in the functioning zone. I knew that I couldn't stop eating altogether and I liked food way too much, but with the restrictions (now gluten and dairy) and being away from home, I didn't eat much. The anxiety skyrocketed and the gut issues increased. I remember sitting in my university dorm room eating sugarless cereal with a tiny spoon so that it would last forever.

New awareness

At 18, I moved cities to finish my degree and finally lived by myself. I started schooling in Child and Youth Care, and for the first time ever, I took some classes on self-reflection. These classes, along with the psychology classes where we learned about Jung and the archetypes and the Collective Unconscious were my favourites, and I felt like I couldn't get enough.

This is when I started to write. I would journal about my progress, or my "aha" moments about myself, or my dreams during these classes. This was the time when I really set foot onto my mythic path. Before, I had just been bumbling along, feeling a ton of anxiety, but not understanding it. I had been using my coping mechanisms and ignoring all of my shadow feelings.

I had decided around the age of six that life had to be shiny; otherwise I wouldn't have the strength to handle it. I gave my power away and essentially made this bargain: "Okay world, I will give up my power and become a good girl and follow the rules, but you must make my life safe and easy because without this power, I can't handle things that are scary or painful.

Basically, I am going to stuff all of my feelings over the next 35 years and be 'good,' because I have learned that my emotions are uncomfortable to others and they are uncomfortable for me. Because I won't be practiced at feeling my emotions, acknowledging the messages behind them, and using them to make changes in my life accordingly, I will not be able to handle them when they feel big and unmanageable. So please, keep the pain to a minimum. Thank you."

But that's not how life works. And the problem with not ever wanting to feel the "bad" emotions is that we don't get to feel the "good" ones either. They all become deadened. Then, one day we wake up and we're 40 and we don't know why we can't feel joy.

When I lost the connection to my power back then, I gave up a platter of joy for a giant platter of "shoulds." I jumped full force onto that train and rode it hard for the next 30 years. The control and competition in me felt the strongest and most comfortable, so I became the nicest, most easy-going "should-er" that you ever did see. It almost broke me. And I spent all those years of my life trying to get it back and find it again. I was so terrified to no longer feel connected to who I was, that I controlled myself and my life as intensely as I could.

Where had my soul gone during this time, you ask? Did she abandon me? Did she just ditch me because I stopped listening to her voice? No, she was still there, pouring love on me every single day, while I wrestled with myself inside my brain. Then, when I was 22, before I got married, my soul got a bit louder — okay, she got really loud!

Wake-up call

It's a Saturday, and my fiancé and I are driving in separate cars to our hometown, two hours away. He's driving his car, which I had been rear-ended in two weeks before by a dump truck.

I had just bought a new car and was driving it home to get something fixed on it. It was one of those west coast winter days, when the rain pummels the earth for hours, and the water starts to pool in mini-lakes and rivers that run across the highway.

I remember driving behind my fiancé and feeling intense anxiety rushing through me at the speed we were going (not fast for a normal day, but too fast in this weather for my comfort). We were in the inside lane and I had a quick flash of intuition to go to the outside lane. I ignored it because I was following my husband-to-be and he would keep me safe . . . or so I told myself.

A second later, an accident flashes through my mind. A second after that, I hit water, panic, and hit the brakes. I spin and hit the cement meridian. I close my eyes and wait for another car to hit me as I spin across two lanes of traffic . . . but nothing . . . and then I hit the ditch.

Gobsmacked that I am still alive, I open my eyes. I open the car door and see my fiancé running in slow motion (or so it seems) toward me. I feel like I'm in a romance movie. He had pulled over when he couldn't see me in his rearview mirror anymore, and is running back to me now.

I feel protected and loved. As he drives me to my parent's house, I feel connected to him in a way that I haven't before. I feel safe and looked after.

But, over the next few years, I have crushing PTSD, my anxiety skyrockets, and I realize that I don't feel safe with him.

That summer, we got married and we both continued going to university . . . and I felt lonely and alone.

Finding truth

The only place I feel any light around me is in this one university class during my third year.

I sit in this counselling class for my Child and Youth Care degree, and I feel something. It's only three hours out of my week, but I carry that feeling that I get in that classroom, with those people, through my whole week — and I tell no one. Well, I try to share the deep insights that I am learning, the self-awareness and connection to myself, with my husband, but all of my built up excitement falls flat.

My energy about all the things I am learning has me vibrating with the magic of it all, but then I come home and tell my husband about it and he pours his doubt all over my passionate fire and I let it fizzle out, meanwhile burning up inside.

I am stumbling across my truth in these classes and it lights me up. I feel something that I haven't felt since I was five. So I carry on with my passionate search for my Wild self. I have gotten a taste of that Wild essence within and I am not about to give it up for someone else's doubt. My own doubt is heavy, but my heart pulls me back to these classes and I carry on, but in secret. And the secrets carry on for many years.

I check all the boxes of society. Unconsciously, I think that if I just do everything right, I won't feel afraid. But that has never worked. The more I shove my Wild self into this "perfect" form, the more I feel abandoned and unsupported.

And this old story and expectation that I have takes me through one experience after another of feeling abandoned.

In addition to feeling unsupported in my marriage, in my "perfect" government job that I get after completing university I feel "not good enough" and unsupported. I am a social worker, which is a career where I give and give and nothing feels like it is really helping others. I feel like I am wrapped up in unending paperwork and computer work, giving energy out and . . . feeling "not good enough."

I keep finding myself in situations where I am trying to feel connected to something, but end up feeling empty instead. And one day I realize that I've been looking everywhere outside myself for support and connection, but I have abandoned myself in pursuit of all societal and familial expectations. I have tried so hard to stuff myself into boxes in an attempt to feel safe, but I end up feeling more and more abandoned and alone. The day I finally quit my job, I walk into my boss's office, sit down and say, "I'm not needed here; I'm needed out there."

I have no idea what I am needed for, but I know with every piece of Wild within me that I can't carry on ignoring myself like this. I can't continue feeling shrivelled inside. It hurts too much to keep stuffing the Wild in me when she is screaming to express herself.

But before I get brave enough to really show my Wildness to the world, I have to go through the biggest hell of my life so far — divorce.

Coming out of hiding: embarking on the soul's journey

"I don't know if I want to be married anymore."

My husband said these words to me as he stood in the doorway on his way out for drinks with a friend. The kids — a girl, five, and a boy, three — my beloved babies, were tucked into bed, dreaming blissfully, as my world started to unravel. After my husband stepped out the door, I collapsed.

"How can this happen? How can nine years of marriage be thrown away just like that?"

It's not as if I hadn't seen the signs. Just two weeks before this statement was uttered, I had been talking to my mom and said, "What am I gonna do? Am I going to have to leave him?"

Things had been really tough. We seemed to argue about everything, and I did not feel emotionally supported by this man, my husband. Plus, I had been hiding who I really was literally and figuratively. I had been hiding my angel cards and stones from him because I didn't think he would accept me for who I was.

When I finally calmed down from the shock of his pronouncement, I gradually started to accept that this was really happening to me. It started to dawn on me that though this seemed like one of the worst things that can happen to someone, it might be a huge gift. Yes, life with a split family was going to hurt a lot. Losing the life I thought I had was going to take a lot of adjustment, letting go, and growth.

But I decided that this might have happened not to me, but for me, so that I could experience freedom. It was in the moment of this shocking, life-changing revelation, that I realized I had always been terrified that a big scary thing might happen in my life, and that I wouldn't be able to handle it.

But now, the big scary thing was happening and I was still alive! In fact, in the days since realizing that I was going to be divorced, I had been feeling more aliveness in my solar plexus than I had felt for a long time. Yes, I was terribly angry, but at least I felt alive. I realized then that trying to live the perfect life with the picket fence and the handsome husband and the two kids and the perfect job had been slowly eating away at my soul.

In the days and months following this crisis, as acceptance of my new life was settling into my mind and awareness, a major shift was happening within me. I knew that if my husband hadn't left, I would probably never have left him, because I believed so strongly in marriage and the importance of being "good" and "doing it right." But now that it was happening and I didn't have any say in the matter, I was embracing my new world, and a quiet strength was growing within me. Even though the tearing apart of my life as I knew it was excruciating, I felt a new space within me opening up. I felt a strong knowing that this was exactly what needed to happen to me at this point in my life. I felt myself moving into this new space and it felt exciting and rich with colour.

It was in those moments after he made his proclamation that my life really changed. It was one of those raw, poignant times where a choice is being made that will change your whole life going forward. It was right then that my life took on a new direction. I picked myself off the floor, stood at the counter in the house we had built together just three years before, and promised myself this: "I am going to be the best and truest version of me that I can be for myself and for my children." And that's what I have been working on ever since.

"One of the most calming and powerful actions you can do to intervene in a stormy world is to stand up and show your Soul. Struggling Souls catch light from other souls who are fully lit and willing to show it." —DR. CLARISSA PINKOLA ESTÉS

My world post-divorce was definitely stormy, but my commitment to diving into my soul and listening to what she was longing for was strong. I made a promise to her that I would slow down and listen to her, no matter how many years it took me. Listening to my soul self became my most important work. I started the journey by searching back into my childhood for the things that I loved to do; things that felt surrounded by joy.

I picked two things that I would do to focus on my healing: yoga teacher training and salsa dancing. Since watching Patrick Swayze and Jennifer Grey in *Dirty Dancing* when I was 11, and after learning every step of their final routine, I was hooked, but partner dancing wasn't really a thing when I grew up — other than learning some square dance and jive in Grade 7, which was a hoot.

So instead, I spent years in jazz dance, hoping to quell my urge for partner dance. It didn't get quelled. So I walked into my first salsa dance lesson all alone, with terror in my stomach and a thrill in my heart.

Dancing with my soul

My soul takes me all the way to New York with dancing.

I am running with a friend one day. She and I dance together and she is coming to New York for a salsa congress with me in a month. As we're running she says nonchalantly, "What would you think of joining a group, working with a top choreographer, and dancing on stage while we're in New York?"

I say, "That's a no."

"Come on, it will be fun!" she keeps trying. I can't even think about the idea without feeling sick, so I tell her we will go to the workshops, but there is no way I'm dancing on stage. I am so wrong.

We arrive in New York on a Thursday and are getting registered for the programs and workshops when my friend walks up to me and says, "Come over here! This is where we sign up for the choreographer I told you about!" It happens so fast and I have this dance adrenaline and confidence running through me so I say, "Ok, I'll come to support you and be with you, but I am not committing to going on stage!"

Well, by the end of the weekend, we were on stage and dancing salsa in front of 3000 people! And it wasn't like we trained for four days straight and then performed. No, we did other workshops, we trained, we partied, we danced socially until 4 AM, we went on a whirlwind tour with a couple of cute medical students in the East Village and returned at 6 AM on Sunday. And then we performed that night.

When we were announced on stage, friends that we were travelling with didn't even know we were performing and were shocked to see us up there all decked out and shaking our stuff! We came off the stage, riding the performance high, hugged a bunch of people while feeling like celebrities in our fake eyelashes and all, then we headed to the airport to take the red-eye flight home.

My 35-year-old body was exhausted, but my little 11-year-old girl soul was thrilled to the gills!

Healing takes us on a journey back to our Wild selves.

—THIRZA VOYSEY

At this time in my life, dancing for me isn't just fun though. There is so much release of grief and pain that happens with the movement and the surrender that dance requires. I know that so much of my Wildness is buried under grief and betrayal, so I use dance to allow my body to open and the energy to flow out, usually accompanied by tears. I learn the Latin dance called Bachata. It's a partner dance that is sensual and slow. It feels good to surrender and fall into the beat of the sweet music. At night, when my kids are asleep in their beds, I shut off the lights in the living room and play Bachata music and dance by myself.

As I flow around the living room, with the music sliding over me from the overhead speakers, I watch the city lights below and I cry. The tears flow down my face as the pain melts away.

And sometimes, we think we're doing what we want, while the universe is bringing us exactly what we need.

—THIRZA VOYSEY

I need to be cracked open. Control has become such a coping mechanism since my young years and was such a bad habit that both my body and my mind are tight. After my first few lessons in Latin dance, I want to be really good, fast. Patience has never been my greatest attribute. So I sign up for private lessons.

When I am in my first lesson, I know that things are going to get harder before they get easier, emotionally, and physically. I don't know just how in my head I am until I am learning to follow in dance. I also don't realize how rigid I am in my mind and body. Everything is about to change. In order to follow softly, I need to be intensely present in my body, something I had not excelled at since I loved to daydream and had a habit of disassociation. I also need to be balanced and centred.

Dance requires me to flow in my body in ways that I haven't before. I have to be so energetically connected to my partner and so feather-like in my presence that I can feel his intention to move in a certain direction. This, to me, this communication without talking, feels like resonance.

This practice melts the need to control out of me. Every time I try to lead — which is a lot — my partner tells me so. It is so important for me to watch myself try to control everything and to learn the magical art of surrender. With these lessons, I become a real salsa dancer. I am a gentle, feather-like dancer and my partners enjoy dancing with me because I am light and centred. Together, we can flow all over the dance floor with the music filling our bodies. We become a third thing. Our dance is a creation all of its own, and it is magic.

This is everything I have wanted. I am touching the Wild in me every time I open and let the music fill me. One evening at a dance, a woman is watching me. She comes up to me afterwards and says that she felt like my soul was dancing. That was everything to me!

Dance has done its job, and I continue to clear my energy body through dance whenever it feels stuck or overwhelmed. And I dance when life feels like it needs a little more magic in it.

Soul craving

"The way to maintain one's connection to the wild is to ask yourself what it is that you want. This is the sorting of the seed from the dirt. One of the most important discriminations we can make in this matter is the difference between things that beckon to us and things that call from our souls. Nowhere can this be seen more clearly than in the choice of mates and lovers. A lover cannot be chosen a la smorgasbord. A lover has to be chosen from soul-craving. To choose just because something mouthwatering stands before you will never satisfy the hunger of the soul-self. And that is what the intuition is for; it is the direct messenger of the soul."

—DR. CLARISSA PINKOLA ESTÉS

I am single for two years and during that time, there are definitely some smorgasbord choices. I allow myself, after being married for nine years and with the same person for 12 years, some freedom to date and enjoy it. I don't get in my head about it or judge myself for some uncharacteristic choices. It is all a necessary part of my journey.

There are so many new people I meet in the dancing world and there are some scrumptious experiences. Without going into too much detail (my kids are going to read this!), dance is sexy, and sharing my kids with their dad half the time has opened up a lot of nights that could be very quiet and lonely, so I fill them with fun. For the lonely heart, having very sensual experiences and opening up to your own sexiness again is medicine for the soul.

After two years of being single and dating, I am talking to my friend from Finland who has moved in with the kids and I to attend university. I tell her that I can feel him coming. She looks at me like I have two heads. Who do I feel coming? My long-term guy, I tell her. I feel him coming. It has been two years since my divorce. Less than one month later, I meet him.

It's a Wednesday, and I have a meeting at Starbucks with a graphic designer whom I have hired to create business cards for me. I walk into Starbucks at 1 PM and see my designer at a table. I notice that someone is with him. I approach and say hi and then I look at his friend. Well, talk about soul craving! I can't think, or make words come clearly out of my mouth. I feel something that day that I have never experienced before. We sit there talking about my business cards while this buzzing travels up and down my spine and into my head. I feel like I'm floating.

I knew right then that something powerful was happening. And so when Patrick asked me to go out with him later that evening with his friends, not wanting to miss an opportunity, I said yes.

Side note on the importance of numbers to me:

Everything really important that has happened to me since 2007 has been related to numbers. I know something is a yes when a number appears, along with a deep intuitive knowing buzz that I get. That seals the deal for me.

The number thing stems from way back when I was 11. I was at a Christmas bazaar. Imagine a school gym with green, red, and gold decorations everywhere, and Christmas music blasting. I was wandering around looking at booth after booth of tacky Christmas things for sale when I saw the cakewalk! I love cake (and games where you can win something as wonderful as a cake), so I dug in my pocket for some tickets, put them in the bin, and found a number to stand on.

The music started and we walked and walked, and while I was walking I had this magic buzzing in my heart; this feeling that something wonderful was happening. The music stopped and they picked numbers out of a hat and announced that the winning number was 11. I looked down and saw that I was standing on number 11! Ever since, I have loved the number 11. She is my guiding light. When 11 shows up in anything, I pay attention.

The day I met Patrick was November 11th. Also known as 11/11! When I realized the morning after our meeting that it had been November 11th when we met, I was sold!

Don't get me wrong, I had a few doubts. He was nothing like my first husband. Nothing. I took that as a good sign, though, and told myself that I would just keep showing up if I kept having that knowing buzz about us. We've been together now 11 years and married for six of those years. I guess the numbers don't lie!

India

"Do you know what India stands for? I'll Never Do It Again." Said by a lady sitting at our table in the dining hall at the ashram.

She giggled as she said this, sitting beside us at dinner on our first night at the ashram. After barely surviving our first three days in India, we agreed with her.

We had arrived in New Delhi at 2 AM after getting sprayed with some kind of disinfectant on the airplane. We hopped in a tuk-tuk to take us to our booked hotel. Patrick, who is a world traveller, swears by booking the first night and figuring it out from there. It's not my way, but I was embracing newness. As somebody with a lot of fear in my life and my upbringing, I decided that I wanted to go to India because it was the place I was most afraid to go. I thought I could have a new experience while following somebody who had done this kind of travelling before. I was sure right about the new experience part!

We fell asleep at about 3 AM in the hotel and were jarred awake at 5:30 AM by a chanting procession in the street outside our window. We knew we had officially landed in India!

I find it amazing how, lying there, I could feel my culture that I had brought with me energetically from Canada, inside me, bumping up against this incredibly contrasting strong energy of Indian culture. I say "bumping up against" because at first it was like that, but by the end, the energy of India and its people had penetrated me and was mixing with my own energy — and it joined me on my path home.

As we walked the streets that morning, I felt the jarring of each of my senses, and as a very sensitive and sheltered individual, I felt myself quickly shutting down from overwhelm. I had my explorer hat on, and my mind wanted to see it all and take it all in, but my body and my energy could only take so much. I knew what a privilege it was that I could go back to the hotel and recharge when things got to be too much.

We decided that day that we would head south first. We had heard about an ashram there that had inspired me and I wanted to go. We booked a flight for the next evening, New Year's Eve, 2011. After a cockroach fell on Patrick's lap out of the ceiling of the plane, we arrived at the airport at 11:45 PM. We walked outside and asked for a driver to take us on the three-hour drive to the ashram. A man stepped forward and we followed him to his car, ready to put our lives in his hands to drive at night in India for three hours. Anyone who has done this knows what I mean!

We started driving and it turned midnight. The driver stopped in the middle of the highway, with lights rushing past us on all sides, so that he could change the CD. Once he had done it, he kept smiling and yelling Happy New Year, Happy New Year! We celebrated with him for a few minutes and then I fell asleep.

When I woke up a few minutes later, Patrick was holding

onto the seat, white-knuckled, his eyes wild with fear. I asked him quietly what was up, as I watched the driver reach behind him and stick a piece of paper into something and then shove the paper up his nose. Patrick whispered that he had been doing this for a while, multiple times, and each time he did it, he would drive faster and more erratically, passing cars and heading straight into oncoming traffic. Patrick figured he was sniffing gas or something. He was most definitely sniffing something, and we had 2 ½ more hours to drive.

We decided to stay in the car because we would be in greater danger on the side of the highway in India, walking in the dark, and my backpack was huge.

When we finally turned off the highway, we entered some back streets. We were really nervous because it didn't seem to be the place an ashram would be, and we weren't sure he even knew where we wanted to go. Things in India sometimes have multiple names and we might have been saying them wrong. Finally, we arrived in front of multiple huge buildings and we knew we had arrived alive! Looking up at these huge buildings at 3 AM with relief and gratitude swelling inside of me, the energy of the place rushed over me, and I knew that I was going to be changed . . . again.

The Wild lives inside of us . . . in our devotion to something greater than ourselves. —THIRZA VOYSEY

At 5 AM the bells rang and we awoke, snuggled together on top of one sleeping bag on a metal bunk bed. I made my way to the bathroom to find a toilet with foot supports made for squatting for full release. The bathroom and beds in the room were very decrepit and surprisingly like a jail cell — not that either of us had ever spent a night in one. We went to the temple to check in and pay our four dollars for the night, and were upgraded to the fancy couples building.

We took our keys and moved our bags to our new room. As we opened the door to our room, we were met with a sparse room with not a single piece of furniture. We had to go and get our sleeping mats from a storage room — and voilà! Our room was ready. We had our own bathroom with a toilet and shower, so it really was luxury and worth the four dollars per night.

The vibration at the ashram was high, yet calm. I felt serene in every cell in my body during my time there, even though there were thousands of people staying there. Many live there, both Westerners and Indian people, and many are travellers. The thing that connected us to each other was the devotion to something greater than ourselves that threaded through our hearts.

Sitting in meditation on the beach at 5:30 PM, with everyone in their ashram whites watching the sunset and the moon rise, changed my perspective on spirituality. As I sat there, I could feel with every cell the deep support and unconditional love I was receiving from the unseen. After a lifetime of confusion about spirituality and God, wrapped up in guilt and fear, I felt settled in the receiving of the source energy flowing through each one of us sitting on those rocks.

After feeling the loving energy within me so intensely for the week and a half that we spent at the ashram, I knew it was something I wanted to keep close to me throughout my days. It wasn't until we returned home to Canada that I felt the great loss of that connection to source, and realized that I would have to cultivate this feeling in my world, halfway around the globe from where I first found it.

Be in harmony with yourself

"To confront a person with their own shadow is to show them their own light." —CARL JUNG

I had never liked anything dark — moods, shows, movies, conversations. Until this point, I was scared of everything other than light. So, after our trip to India, I spent the next five years working on clearing out my energy centres so that I could be shiny and light.

I took my yoga teacher training. The class about the energy centres, called chakras in the yogic tradition, had drawn me down a fascinating rabbit hole. I was in awe of these energetic centres, and felt that same vibration within me that I have come to recognize as my intuition telling me to pay attention because something is important. I felt like learning about them would change my life entirely, so I dedicated myself to learning everything I possibly could about them.

I knew that this knowledge of the energy centres was going to be a huge part of my work and my healing and my schooling on this earth. Of course, I didn't see how, but like with all things that come forward and fill my heart with bubbles of excitement, I knew their importance and deep wisdom for my path. The wisdom and learning of energy centres is a fascinating subject that one can learn about for one's entire life.

The energy centres (chakras) really are everything. They explain how we interact with the world around us and within us and why we do so. They hold both our light and our shadow selves. Through this work, I knew I would be forced to face my shadow self. When I want to learn something, I research it like crazy, live it, and then I often teach it. So in true Thirza fashion, once I received my 200 hour yoga teacher training, I started offering courses about the energy centres, mixed with yoga and meditation.

I called my first course "A Radiant Mess." This is an 8-week course in which we dive into the energy centres, one per week. Because each energy centre corresponds both physically with the body and with levels of consciousness, we envelope ourselves in the energy of that centre for an entire week.

For example, the energy of the first energy centre or root chakra in the yogic tradition, is about our roots — our family of origin, our first seven years of development as a child, our grounding to the earth, our physical body, our structural system. This energy centre is about feeling supported on this earth and trusting that we are safe and provided for. It's easy to see that this is something not felt by the collective of our society. So we spend this week as a group, going through or "marinating," as I like to say, in the energies of this centre. The root chakra week brings up a lot of belief systems that we have lived under forever, but that might be ready to be challenged or reevaluated.

As the teacher, even though I have gone through this course many times over with my clients and groups, I still go through the experiences of the centres every dang time I run the course. I love it. It makes me feel connected to who I really am and to the light that runs through me. Basically, what is happening in these courses, is that we are going through our own being and shining it up so that it's all nice and shiny like a prism. When our energy centres are clear and free of old muck and yuck from our traumas or experiences in childhood, our worlds can and will be full of joy, wellbeing, wealth, health, and bliss.

Seeing the world through the lens of the energy centres and their levels of consciousness, or truths, has stayed with me through my entire adult life in business and in life. It has been the theme that runs through all that I teach and create. I have found that the most beneficial thing we can do to improve our own lives and to heal is to align and clear our energy centres. I have devoted my life to this and the energy work has shown up in so many fun forms!

The nervous system

I was never diagnosed with PTSD and I was never abused. I have, however, lived a life of fear, with an extended flight-or-fight response, which has contributed to high levels of cortisol often running through my body. This has made me feel like my nerves are raw, and I react with a high level of stress for things that are not such a big deal. This keeps my body tight, my brain on high alert, and my digestion sluggish.

The fear keeps me out of alignment with who I really am. I know what the issue is intellectually. As a social worker, I could just rationalize and "fix" problems for others — but not for myself. I know lots of things intellectually.

I'm a Gemini, the Twins. True to my nature, I like to devour nonfiction books. I have read the odd fiction book in my life, but over the past few years, if it's not a memoir, or nonfiction, I'm not interested. This obsession with information has served me well, but lately I have stumbled upon things that I just can't quite intellectualize away, things like chronic stomach pain and digestive issues. Things like waking up in a sweat with the feeling of my energy dropping out of the bottom of my feet. Things like high anxiety and panic for no apparent reason.

Be Raw Chocolate

Patrick and I had a son, Kai, and when he was two years old, I started making raw chocolate in the kitchen. I love chocolate and was looking for a way to make it as healthy as possible — of course! I also wanted to somehow bring my healing work into it. This wasn't a fine-tuned plan. All I was doing was following the bubbles in my heart. I found a woman who showed me how to make raw chocolate, and . . . this was the beginning of something big. I could feel it!

I started making the chocolate for myself and my family. Then one day, I was on a walk with my wiener dog, Zen. I always get my best ideas or realizations on walks, and this time was no different. I was walking along when a fully formed idea dropped into my awareness. The idea was to make seven flavours of chocolate bars and have them correspond to the seven energy centres. Of course! I started dreaming up ideas for flavours and names, and by the time I returned home, I had seven flavours! I presented the idea to my hubby, a graphic designer extraordinaire, who loved it and started designing the boxes.

I entered a Christmas craft fair that was big in the area. By November, I was in full production, making batch after batch of raw chocolate that barely made it into the packaging because it was so yummy! I mean seriously, I was eating all my profits!

The weekend of the market came and I was cutting the packages by hand with an exacto knife — a very painstaking job! The market was four days long. I had to go home and make more chocolate after the first two days because I had sold so much! This market was very indicative of where the business was going. Also, I met a woman at that market who had a very big role in our eventually moving to our farm and island home. Oh, it's all linked when we start to pay attention!

A few weeks after the market, a friend of my mom's contacted me, wanting to meet to discuss my business. She offered to become an investor or partner. She was very open to what I wanted to do and thought it would be fun to be involved. We became business partners and created an approved kitchen in her basement suite after many other options fell through. We hired people and I taught them to make the chocolate. I had a goal to make our chocolate the most healing it could possibly be.

The Goddess of Cacao and I had a chat about the healing coming out of the rainforest and wanting to carry the energy of love around the world. I was up for that assignment! Cacao has a very high vibration as a food, and in addition, I was inspired to infuse each batch with healing as it was tempering.

Tempering is basically a heating and cooling process that allows the cells within the chocolate to become solidified so that it doesn't melt at room temperature. Of course with raw chocolate, the temperature has to be very exact to keep the aliveness of the raw cacao, which is a fermented food and so full of good stuff! I intuited that we would infuse it with healing while the chocolate was "resting" after the heating and cooling, and just before the flavours were added and it was poured into molds.

We had multiple people who sampled the chocolate ask, "Do you put something in this? I can feel it more than I can even taste it, and it feels amazing!"

"That's love you're feeling," I would say! I loved spending those two years bringing the chocolate to people all across the country and watching their faces relax and their eyes close as they ate it, or watching their eyes roll up into their heads because they were enjoying the experience so thoroughly. I mean, that's how great I feel when I eat it, which is why I continue to eat it every single day!

In 2015, after going to big food shows across the country and having our food distributed through a Canadian distributor to all the health food stores, my business partner came to me and said she was ready to back out of the business. She had enjoyed herself fully but needed to move on to other things. I had been feeling like we had grown as much as possible within the country and it was time to go to the USA, but that felt big and intimidating. It also felt like it was time for a different facility and I wasn't ready to sink a bunch more money into the business, so we decided to look for a buyer.

It wasn't long before we found a buyer in Toronto. We sold the business and wrapped everything up. The only thing left was to travel to Toronto from the west coast to teach them how to make the chocolate and how to do the healings.

I felt a lot of things about letting go of the business, but I knew I was ready to move on. The biggest thing I wanted out of this was for the business and the bars to carry on and keep living as a creation.

In the summer of that year, we flew to Montreal to visit my hubby's family and meet up with friends. After a wonderful summer touristy visit to Montreal, I took the train to Toronto for a few days to teach chocolate making to the people who had purchased the business.

What a weird experience that was! I was led into a huge warehouse with a little hot plate and makeshift counter in the corner. A bunch of workers were gathered around, ready and eager to learn the art of chocolate making. I taught them over a period of three days, and by the end, they were starting to talk about their own flavour ideas to add to the list.

They were excited and ready to start making their own chocolate to carry on the business. We had given them a bunch of inventory so they won't have to actually make any more for a few months. I left with hope in my heart and money in my pockets (well, a bit of money; the profits were not great after all was said and done, but I did create myself a job for two years and come out with a little bit in the end).

But I was not convinced that the business would continue. I watched the stores at home for a few months and they continued to carry the Be Raw Chocolate bars . . . but then they stopped and I never saw them again.

It felt sad to see something end that had brought so much joy to the country and beyond. I know that there are other companies making raw chocolate, but not like we did. Not with the same intentions we did. Not with the energy of love and healing so deeply infused into the chocolate . . . that's not true I'm sure. There are so many amazing chocolate bars out there that are heavenly. I have since checked. But you get where I was coming from: I was sad and felt an ending that maybe I wasn't really ready for.

But in true Me-style, I carried on with gusto to the next thing. And I didn't know it then, but the next thing was going to rock my world so greatly and call so much courage and strength from me that I may not have entered into it had I known at the time . . . but isn't that the best? The not-knowing, the ignorance with which we dive head first into things that feel right, and then pick up the pieces after? It's my favourite way to go — ask my family.

Returning to horses

Horses marched back into my life under the guise of "fun and bonding" with my daughter. She was 10, and we decided to start her in pony club every Sunday at a ranch nearby. She learned to clean the barn, tack the horses up, and she had a riding lesson or went for a trail ride every week.

I loved the excuse to hang out every Sunday with the horses and my daughter in our blissful place. During this time, she was going through some high anxiety and fear. She was doing talk therapy, but wasn't finding it very helpful. When we were with the horses though, she was totally different. It was like she was a different person. She would seem like a queen up there on her horse. There was no fear in her body, just bliss.

This connection and confidence was really accentuated and apparent to me on a trail ride at the ranch one day. I would often ride with her when she wanted a trail ride instead of a lesson. As we got the horses ready, I could hear dirt bikes on the trails where we were going to be riding. I expressed my worry about this to my daughter and I felt the fear running through my body as I did. I tacked my horse up in a nervous flurry and we headed out.

During the ride, every time I heard the bikes, I tensed, and mentioned my fear. My daughter was annoyed by my perseverating and told me as much. I can't say I blame her.

She said to me, "Why are you so scared? You know your horse can feel your fear, right?" I knew, but I couldn't help myself. My mind kept playing scary situations that involved our horses spooking and dumping us on the ground. I had to worry about not just one of us during our rides, but both of us. Our ride turned out to be fine other than my inability to relax the whole time. It wasn't until we got back to the field that things went sideways.

We entered the ranch through the back gate. She went first on her horse and I followed. I had gotten off my horse to open and shut the gate. I then stood on a stump and brought my horse alongside so that I could get on her back. I put my foot in one stirrup and as I went to swing my other leg over her back, she took off, bucking and farting down the field as I landed with a painful thud on the ground on my butt.

My daughter, worried about me, turned her horse around and came back to check on me. She made sure I was okay and then went on to tell me how much my horse didn't like my freaky vibe on her back. I was humiliated. My body and my ego were severely bruised and I was terrified. There was no way I was going to get back on her like my daughter suggested. I was standing face-to-face with my own shadow and I sure didn't like what I saw.

At the time I didn't know what the horse was doing. I knew she didn't like my freaky vibe, but instead of having the awareness that she was trying to lead me to my own light and show me what wasn't working in my life, I just felt like she hated me and wanted me off. This was my first real introduction to the magical wisdom and high vibration of horses. And it was about to get a lot more interesting.

The Medicine Horses

It was shortly after this encounter that I met the Medicine Horses and their humans. It was through meeting this herd of horses that I realized just how much spiritual work the horses were doing with us humans.

A year or two after my daughter started pony club, she was still experiencing anxiety, and it was getting really hard for our family, and extremely hard for her. She continued to receive therapy, and I continued to look for an alternative therapy that would help as well. We tried hypnotherapy, which she disliked, and then one day a friend called to ask me about some yoga ideas for a friend. During the conversation, she dropped a few sentences about a medicine horse farm she had gone to. Wait, what?

We got off the phone, and with my heart pounding in my chest, I called the farm and booked an appointment for us. I knew there was going to be so much in this meeting for me too.

My daughter and I arrived at the farm and walked straight to the horse field. We saw horses grazing in one big field, with a horse-sized labyrinth in the middle. We were led out to meet the horses by the woman who partners with the horses for healing work.

We each picked a horse to work with, and we walked them through the labyrinth. We were instructed to let go of anything we no longer needed to carry around with us in our minds. Then we each had our own little session with our horse. After we walked the labyrinth and had some meditation time at the centre, my daughter went off to the round pen with the woman and one of the horses. They chatted for a while and did some more work before I was invited into the round pen. We were going to make some bracelets out of horse mane. We proceeded to ask the horses if they were okay with us taking some hair from their manes and tails for bracelets (we didn't need much). They were gracious and stood still while we collected hair. We then braided our bracelets and put them on our wrists, weaving our wishes for ourselves into them. When we left, we thanked everyone and promised we would be back to visit.

The entire experience was deeply spiritual for me. I felt something beyond anything I had ever felt with nature, land, and horses. I always knew there was something magical, but I had never felt it so fully in my body. I felt a power after the session that has stayed with me, and I love to wear my horse hair bracelet to remind me of the freedom and power that horses represent to me.

After this transformational experience with the herd, I knew that my life was changing in a big way and this was as terrifying as it was exciting. As with when I met my husband, I felt a shift coming. I get this intuitive sense often, and it's always a little unsettling — or a lot unsettling! It feels like I'm standing on the edge of a cliff about to jump, hoping and trusting that the universe will build a bridge under me to support me so I don't fall.

Sometimes it feels like I'm standing at the edge of the wild ocean on a foggy day. The ocean feels like my future full of wisdom, but I can't see anything in it because of the storm, so all I can do is take one step at a time and see one foot in front of me as I walk in.

It's kind of a crazy way to live, following these impulses, but I have learned since my soul-following-journey started after my divorce, that my soul gives me feelings in my body to follow that feel like "yes" — or sometimes I get messages through numbers or symbols. And when I recognize that "yes," the only thing to do is follow and trust. When I lose faith I need to keep going, reminding myself that I was led here, and keep trusting. This Wild instinctual way of living has never steered me wrong yet.

Do I have doubts, you ask? Yes, I have doubts. I have doubts about following the Wild soul way but whenever I do, I remind myself that *Abraham-Hicks* says that everything works out in the end, and if it hasn't worked out yet, it's not the end!

Searching for Soulfarm

Shortly after I had the epiphany that my future was going to include horses for life and work, I knew that we had to move. We were living in an older, renovated home in the city and we obviously needed a farm . . . and some horses! That sounds like a huge leap for any family, and it most definitely was for ours. Since the kids were six and four years old, we had shared them with their dad one week on/one week off, and then two weeks on/two weeks off.

Now they were 15 and 13, and things were really about to change! We had started looking for property the year before so that we could grow our own food. We had been growing vegetables and fruit in raised beds, filling our little city yard. It was when my husband burst into the front yard and filled the grass with raised beds and started lasagna gardening that we realized it was time to move.

I was more than keen and had always wanted to live on a farm, but I hadn't told Patrick my tentative decision about the horses yet. Property searches hadn't been very fruitful so far.

Don't get me wrong; I love house-hunting. It could easily become an obsession of mine, but it can be a very emotionally up-and-down experience when you're looking for your next family home and nothing is showing up.

For someone who really doesn't have much patience, when I know that I've thrown something out to the world to be manifested and I can feel it's on its way, I possess a surprising amount of patience. Well, sometimes. As long as it is not about getting a new horse!

At one point we thought we had found a place, but then something didn't feel right and so we ended the process. All of the houses we got close to buying during that time, when I got really real with myself, felt like another stopover before we found our forever home.

"The Soul of the Land can best be felt through the soles of the feet."
—WILD WOMAN SISTERHOOD

We hadn't planned to move to a little Gulf Island, but it was definitely in our hearts for a long time. For many years, my parents have had a cabin on a little tiny island in the bay of the city we lived in, and every single time I stepped off the boat onto the island, I didn't want to leave. I used to ignore this feeling or call it silly, or think, "Everyone feels these things but it's not realistic for you," but this time, since I was committed to my soul's journey, I paid attention.

We had come to what is now our island a few times to look at houses over the years and each time, our hearts exploded open, but each time we scratched it out as an option because the big kids would have to take the ferry to school. But this time we booked a few houses to look at, and one piece of land that didn't have a house on it. I had said to my husband a few weeks before, "I feel like we might build. You're a designer, so you should build your own house!" (I had already built one house with my "wuzband," so I was ok with it). He argued that he wasn't ready for that kind of responsibility and expense, but he agreed to look at this one property at the end of our day.

As we walk onto the property, I feel my heart buzzing. I feel like I'm walking into my future. The curved driveway opens up to a funky little barn with two outdoor stalls, and I imagine my horses standing there munching their hay.

There are sheep here and they are now wandering around pooping everywhere. I can feel the soul of the land speaking to me and holding me. I can hear horses whispering to me of adventures and healing and sharing the ways I know, the land speaks to me of my own Wildness. My husband says later that he tried to hate it, but he loved it and felt that same connection that I felt. It's going to be ours! We go home and now we have to make an offer on the land, so we do it that same night. There are two other offers on the land so we offer the full price. And then we wait.

At about 10 o'clock that night, we hear that we got the place. It's all happening so fast! That night I barely sleep. I roll around all night thinking about this huge choice that we are making and how crazy it seems. I have so many "what ifs" and "yeah buts." What if my big kids hate it and choose to live with their dad full-time? What if they hate me? What if they think I have ruined their lives?

The guilt and the worry and fear are pushing down on my lungs throughout the night. By morning I don't feel any better and worry that I might have made the biggest mistake of my life!

I roll over and face my husband, ready to bombard him with my regrets and fears and a story about why I am done with this whole cockamamie plan.

He looks at me and says, "No we did not make a big mistake. You pulled me along with you on this plan and you convinced me it was a great plan. So we are doing it and everything will work out. It's going to be amazing!" So we get out of bed and tell the kids that we have decided on a plan. To confirm all my greatest fears, my oldest son, the middle child chill guy says, "No mom, I don't want to move to a little island. You knew that I didn't want that." The guilt of going ahead against what he wanted was so heavy on me, I thought I might break.

The only thing that kept me moving forward, with a deep inner knowing that I still hold today, was that this move wasn't just for me and my soul's journey, it was for all five of us. And so, holding this knowing close to my heart, we move forward with the land. I am prepared to move through all the stages of grief, letting go of my old life to embrace a new life for our whole family.

I knew it would be different, and maybe a really hard change in many ways, but I knew that it was going to be healing for everyone involved. When you feel like the choices you're making for your family might result in unwanted experiences, like my teens not wanting to live with us part-time anymore and choosing to be more often at their dad's house, it takes immense courage and trust to move forward through the fear. I didn't feel like I had these qualities, but my soul did and so I let her take the lead.

And so take the lead she did — and away she went! She grabbed us by the scruff of the neck and led us forward. She helped us sell our house in the city in four days, took us to live at my parents' house on another little island, and helped us to build our modern farmhouse dream on this property.

I used to be told by shamans and healers that I carried cement blocks of responsibility on my shoulders. Since moving into a trailer on the property in July of the year that we built our house, I have felt my energetically heavy responsibility slowly melting away into the earth. This space, this land, holds me and allows for the shedding of all that I no longer am. This shedding and releasing has happened not overnight, but continually over the past four years.

And the kids? Well, my daughter continued to go back and forth between our place and her dad's house, some days happy to experience this new life and sometimes not. My older son chose to be mostly at his dad's, and continues to "hate the island," but we are deeply connected, and he comes often, and we talk every day. He is forgiving me, but missing our old house in the city. Our youngest son loves his island life. He has become farm boy/ island boy easily and loves his life of deep nature immersion. We'll see how it goes when he becomes a teenager.

I have realized through this process that pre-divorce-me would have turned myself inside out to please my children and to create the "perfect" life for them. But when life gave me divorce, I knew at that moment that the only touchstone I had moving forward was my own soul's wishes, which were written in my heart. And so that is how I have made hard choices such as these. If something feels right for me inside my heart, I jump and trust. That's all I can do, because I know that is my soul's path. I know that healing my own self is the best thing that I can do for my children.

If you don't live on a small island, you probably haven't experienced the feeling of driving off the ferry and feeling the island embrace you in a hug. Our home island is right across the bay from a small city, so after spending a day there and returning home, that's what it feels like.

The Embrace of an Island

As I set foot on her off the water,
she wraps her strong arms around me
The day washes away
As I sink back into the embrace of the island.

Islands feel different
They connect us deep below the water
into the centre of the earth.
We are reconnected to the depth of us
when we are here.

We learn to carry this depth within us
It touches the world when we drift away from here
And is renewed each time we return.

The embrace of an island
Isn't like a hug
It's like a deep body massage
And an inner pulling back to home.

—THIRZA VOYSEY

Raven

Raven is the Bringer of Magic. Raven is the messenger of the void, where the great mystery lives. She takes our prayers to where they need to go and brings us messages from our soul.

Raven, the horse, came to me on a day in late May. I had all these specifications about the horse I wanted so that I would get this elusive "right" horse, but I knew deep inside that it would be like it was with my husband. I would just know from the first moment. And I did.

I went to meet her with my mom, which is kind of weird, because my mom isn't much of a horse person and definitely didn't think I needed to get a horse at that time in my life, but she was there. "Cowgirl" was Raven's name at the time. She looked over at us from the field when we stepped out of the car and I knew she was a queen. It wasn't something I could verbalize, but I knew it. My daughter is a queen and she had a very similar energy. She carried herself with a knowing that she is worthy of the best treatment and that we had better figure that out fast.

When we went into her field with her, she kept circling the brushes that we had brought to groom her with, and I realized at that moment that this was going to be an interesting relationship, one where she put ideas into my head and I wouldn't know whether I had created them or whether she had planted them there. I decided it didn't matter, because this is the grey line between us and all unseen energies, so what's the difference if the same thing happens with my horse? Actually, I was giddy.

After we left, I couldn't think of anything else. All I could think about was how she had sashayed toward me with an air of grace, in full connection with who she really is, with her inner being, her soul. This is something I wanted, and she was the one I wanted to do it with.

She arrived at our island on my birthday, June 8, 2017. At 41, after a lifetime of not even dreaming about it because it seemed such a crazy idea, I became a Horse Mama! What an amazing moment it was when she walked out of the trailer in all her bigness (she is 16 hands high, which for those who don't know, is a big-ass horse), and locked those big deep eyes with mine. I was in LOVE.

Raven found her way to me for reasons beyond what I can yet fully understand. There is something in her that mirrors me and something in me that she was obviously drawn to. When I met her, she seemed lonely. As I mentioned, one of the first things she did when my mom and I went to visit her was to circle the brushes for grooming as if to say, "Okay ladies, get to work!" So we did. As she stood in that field alone, neighing for her sheep herd that had been recently moved to a different field, I knew she was a mare who knew her worth. I saw her as the beautiful queen who would stand for nothing less than wonderful treatment. What I didn't see on that day, though, was her ability to see the highest potential of everyone, but I think I intuitively felt it.

Since that day, I have discovered this in all of the work we have done with others and also in what she has taught me. She has kicked my ass, essentially, to be in alignment with who I am. She wants me shining to the world all of my light and hiding none out of fear. Hiding doesn't make sense to her, and she has pushed me in her subtle but not-subtle-big-black-mare-way to stand in my power.

There has also been a theme in the women that have come to work with us here over the past year. They are all women who have great power but don't necessarily see it yet and are not fully embodying it. Sometimes there are situations where people are not fully in their bodies energetically and she lets them know. In simple horse language, she conveys the messages for the humans on our path forward.

Sometimes her message is, "You need to ground yourself often," sometimes it's "Be in your body," or "Set boundaries for yourself," and always her message is "Rock who you are," and "You are worthy." There is no person who has come to the farm, forged a connection with Raven, and not felt this message in a strong way.

Raven and I are very alike in this way. She and I both see the highest selves of people and want to act like a pitbull to get them to rise to it. I am learning much from her around this, though.

When I do a tarot reading for people, I see the highest version of them. I see their potential. A friend of mine came to me for a reading and said, "My biggest dream, honestly, is to be a famous artist." That struck me as odd because I was already seeing her as a famous artist.

A trait that Raven embodies that I do not always have is endless patience. This shows up later as one of the many things I have learned from her. She has stood by the entire time that we have known each other, waiting for me to get my act together or not. She holds her vision of who I am and I work daily to rise to it — or more specifically, to drop all of those belief systems and issues that keep me from rising to it. Her patience is endless (although not when it comes to being fed). She holds a powerful space for us to rise to meet our highest selves, and she has no need to rush that process. She'll just be there eating hay while we figure it out . . .

The night that Raven arrived, and for many nights after that, in my hours of anxiety (around 4 AM - 6 AM), I was hit by waves of love mixed with thoughts like, "Who do I think I am," and "What do I think I'm doing," and "I don't know anything about owning a horse and what if I can't keep her alive?" Let's just say there wasn't a lot of sleep for a few days.

I was used to this type of anxiety, though. I have made many decisions recently that make me feel like I am dangling from a branch, naked, with everything flapping in the wind, hanging over the edge of a cliff. Not a comfortable place to be.

The reason for these many experiences of feeling out of my comfort zone is this: I have a VERY LOUD SOUL. My company, Soulfarm Healing Company, is all about helping people become deeply connected to their authentic selves and to begin to hear their soul and what it wants. The thing about me, though, is that my soul is so dang LOUD! She screams at me and demands things pretty much now! And if I don't listen? Ooh watch out!

So when we bought this farm property, I panicked, even though it was exactly what I needed to be doing and exactly what she (my soul) wanted. When I got a horse, I panicked even though I knew it was exactly what I wanted. You see, there is rarely remorse or "I shouldn't have," or "I don't wanna do this." There is just "What have I done?" and "Who do I think I am?" and basic unworthiness stuff. I realized the other day, pretty much in a smack upside the head, that the almost 30 years of gut/digestive issues that I have had, have been directly related to me feeling not good enough and not believing in the bigness of who I am — of not owning my power. My power and my knowing, frankly, scared the crap right out of me.

Moving to the farm

My youngest son and I moved to the farm to supervise the building of our new house and to be with Raven who was already on the island. She was being boarded at a new friend's home near the ferry. I decided I wanted to be on the land for the whole summer. My husband needed to stay where we were living because he needed Wi-Fi for his business every day. So just like someone always looking for adventure would, I moved my youngest son and I to the farm, along with our new-to-us farm dog, Izzy, and our little wiener dog, Zen. The cat stayed with Patrick and the big kids came and went from their dad's place.

Kai and I lived in my uncle's very old trailer that he lent to us for the occasion. Had I known exactly how this time would have gone, I may not have decided to do the move until November when the house was built. Had I had patience, things would have been easier, but definitely not as adventurous and fun!

We slept in the tent most of the summer and moved into the trailer as the nights got colder. I adored that summer of sleeping under the stars every single night with no Wi-Fi. The big kids brought their friends and tented or slept in the trailer. We moved Raven to the farm, so we slept right beside her paddock and could hear her snorting, whinnying, and breathing. I loved all of it. I even loved having to go to a generous friend's place to use his outdoor shower. I loved the whining that my teenagers did every time we had to go for a shower and do it outside!

When September came and I had to get my youngest son to kindergarten and the older ones had to go to high school, things definitely got more difficult — and emotional. Here is a blog post that I wrote in September of that year that shows the feeling of what was happening at the time.

Fall arrives

Ahhh, the building of Soulfarm continues and I am sitting in a Rubbermaid container, having my bath. Today is the three-month anniversary of living on this land in a trailer and tent with my youngest son. I am amazed we have survived this adventure this long and with less than a month before I am in my house (here's to hoping!), I am feeling excitement, awe, a little anxiety and still a little turmoil.

I have been shedding the fear and anxiety hard and fast since living on this land (it is amazing how in tune with nature one becomes when sleeping in a trailer or tent, hearing the sounds of the land all night long). And then there is Raven, the black horse, who lives right outside the trailer. We can hear the vibration on the earth as she walks back and forth. Thank goodness at night, everyone is mostly silent. The dogs sleep, my son sleeps, the horse sleeps, I usually sleep, but not that owl.

He mostly calls with his young-girl-screaming sound, followed by the question of, "Who, who, who?" He always wakes me, usually with a start, and then I am soothed back to sleep by the gentle, repetitive sounds of him calling in the night.

We saw him one night from the tent. At dusk, we could see his shape perched on a branch. It was our first sighting of him and we were unconvinced. After a few seconds, he expanded his great wings and flew straight by us. The silhouette against the almost dark sky was undeniably an owl. Owls are all about helping us see in the dark. They are about using our senses of clairvoyance and clairaudience, seeing beyond what is physical and hearing beyond. They also help us to see that which people are hiding from themselves and others. Essentially seeing the shadow.

I find this is something I work with a lot in my tarot readings. I am not there to help people know that they might meet someone or win the lottery (although these things sometimes come up — well not the lottery one yet). Instead, the readings are to help people become more in line with their soul. We do a general reading to see where that person is at and what sorts of issues they are dealing with, then we dig right into soul work.

We look at the chakras, or energy centres, to see where there are energetic blocks in their life or body that may be keeping their dreams from them. We then can see solutions for helping them melt these blockages and allow their energy to flow again, which will in turn bring what they want to them. Raven, the Medicine Horse, then helps further balance and release energy within the person's body.

Owl helps with these readings by revealing the unseen. There are often elements that people don't want to face directly or are scared to face. Owl also leads us through the tunnel of darkness to the light on the other side. I saw this play out one day recently when I was having a really tough day. I was pre-menstrual and feeling overwhelmed. Kai woke up happy, but then felt my turmoil and turned quickly into a clingy, crying mess.

We went to school, and after a week and a half of great drop-offs and no crying, he clung to me like a koala bear, terrified that I might leave him. I, of course, was not feeling the strength to just walk out, so I hung around like a lost puppy and got hug after hug from friendly island strangers. I finally pulled myself out of there, content that my little man would be okay, and drove home. I phoned my hubby and bawled to him about all the things that were weighing on me: that our house was never going to get finished, that our teenagers were never going to come live with us again because they don't want to live here, that it was going to rain for the rest of the winter and I was going to freeze, and on and on.

Not only was I crying and driving, but I was trying to cry to my husband on speaker phone, but he couldn't hear me because the service kept cutting out. I gave up trying to talk to him with tears streaming down my face (very unsafe driving) and saw something out of the corner of my eye. It was an owl. It landed on the fence on the side of the road. I pulled over and it was right beside my passenger window. It stared right into the window at me for a full two minutes, with its big black beady eyes looking right into me. After it flew away, I went home and looked into my information about Owl. The first line I saw was, "Owl leads you through the dark tunnel and into the light." Ahhh . . . peace again. Thank you Owl!

One year at Soulfarm

Tonight marks one year since we moved to Soulfarm. I just finished saying to my husband, "This has been the wildest, most amazing year of my life. I have grown so much since we moved here a year ago." This is so true. I've had breakthrough after breakthrough. How does this happen after a life of chronic worry, anxiety, constant thinking, and health issues? How is it that I've come to this place where I feel so alive? So new and reborn?

As I lay there in bed earlier I saw the creation of this book, this story about Soulfarm. Years ago we picked the name Soulfarm on a trip to Tofino, a little surfer town on the west coast of Vancouver Island. Patrick and I were driving and talking about ideas of names for things — namely his beard oil and my chakra classes. We came up with Manfur and Soulfarm respectively. Both names have stuck — and they rock, if I do say so myself.

But Soulfarm was meant to be a farm and we didn't have a farm yet. I had been starting to dream of a place where we could grow food and have animals, but it wasn't even a full dream yet, just a name.

But as it is with dreams, you just hold them lightly in your mind like you would hold a butterfly in your hand and allow it to do what it does. Dreams, if left to their own devices, will surely flourish. If we don't shove them into boxes and beat on them with "shoulds" and "can'ts," they quietly grow. And like a fuzzy dandelion seed, they take off and catch on the wind to fly.

What an exciting adventure this has been, one that I was not at all prepared for. I was still so much the old me. I was so tied up with guilt and shame and indecision and uncertainty about this move that the only thing I had as a lifeline was that I knew it was part of my path.

My heart, she had drawn me here, while my loud, obstinate soul demanded that I listen to her, and together they dragged me here by the hair. That's it! They were in cahoots and I was merely their pawn . . . and that's how things are.

Piper comes

Nothing about any horse that I have gotten (now that we're three horses in), makes logical sense. The horses don't operate in that world, and I have realized that despite years of trying to prove to the world that I can, I admit that I don't either. The horse world and timing is magical, and is often for the highest good for everyone involved, and we don't usually (or ever) have all the pieces of information — and that is how it should be. So all we can do is trust.

I had been saying for a long while that Raven needed a buddy. I knew from watching her and listening to her that she was not a lone horse. Are there any horses that really thrive alone? I would say that as herd animals, no. Maybe there are a few that seem to, but truth be told, they always are happier with other horses. I had been "trying" in the physical world to get a young mare from a rescue. The day she was going to come, it was reported to me that she "refused" to get on the truck (the woman who ran the place was at work and unable to help). As we were leaving within two weeks for a holiday, I had no choice but to suggest we wait until the new year.

I surrendered and told Source that I was giving up and that Raven would have to be by herself with the goats while we were away and until we could find her a friend. That night, I had a dream about a dark horse with a white blaze and brown muzzle. I saw him as clearly in my dream as I now see him standing before me. The next day, a friend posted on my feed about a horse who was about 28 and looking for a retirement home. I wouldn't have looked at him, because he had to come across a couple of ferries, but I had dreamt about him. I contacted the woman and tried to hold her off because we were going away soon, but she offered to bring him in two days. Well, it was decided. Piper was coming to live at Soulfarm.

The woman told me that Piper wasn't much of a "horse" horse. She told me that he loved having one human that he bonds to. She said every time they tried to put him in a field with other horses, he just stood and whinnied or paced at the fence.

Well, the day for him to arrive came quickly and we were ready. I had Raven in a field and the gate closed for their introduction. Piper got off the truck and went straight to the fence where she was. They sniffed each other and made a couple of squeals. Within minutes, they were both eating calmly, so I put them together in the field. I couldn't believe it! Raven is a pretty chilled out horse and has been with many horses before with no problem, but I couldn't believe how quickly they were happy together and very bonded. He likes us humans and does amazing work with people, but the depth to which he has bonded with Raven is beautiful. And so they shall live happily together until the end of their days.

Piper helps people with their higher energy centres, namely the 5th, 6th, and 7th (throat, third eye, and crown), and also high heart. He helps humans to see that they need to shift into living with integrity, making their words and actions match their beliefs. He helps people understand what their soul purpose is and holds space for them to move towards it. As with all of them, he is an intense heart healer. I have seen him soothe people who were anywhere from extremely anxious to dissociative, and help them to get back into their bodies. He loves hanging out and receiving and giving energy work.

There are so many kinds of healers. Piper, with his strong gentleness and his nourishing energy is one, while right beside him can be another horse with her powerful need to connect us with our gifts and help us unearth anything in our shadow. That horse is Luna.

Luna

The day I purchased Luna from an auction unknowingly, I knew another major transition was happening for me. It was a regular Saturday. For a few months, I had been putting out to the universe that I was looking for a riding horse for kids (after finally convincing my hubby of course).

I had noticed that Raven wasn't the most thrilled about doing the kids' lessons and so I was calling in a "child safe" horse.

As I do with these sorts of "universe requests," I had put it out there and then kind of let it be (often with houses or horses I can get in the way with too much looking and trying and deciding), but this time I was pretty focused on other things while I allowed this to happen.

So, on this particular Saturday morning, we had a friend staying and I had a photoshoot booked for the afternoon. Normally, these two things would have kept me plenty busy and focused enough to not accomplish anything else, but when the universe is working for you, time is kind of irrelevant.

It went like this: As I was getting ready for the day, I looked at my phone for a minute. Scrolling through, I came across a group that follows horse auctions and there was one that day. So I was thinking of sending a quick message off to this woman and all of a sudden I was butt-dialing her!

I would never normally have called this woman directly. I had always emailed her in the past, but here I was with the phone ringing in my hand!

She then gave me the number for the man who was covering the auction.

All of a sudden, I'm talking to the man who is at the auction like I'm some kind of auction-buying horse-woman! He's asking what I'm looking for in a horse and telling me that I should send my maximum bid as an e-transfer.

I found myself way too deep into this conversation for my own comfort. I told him that I wasn't ready to commit or send money, but he could send me a message with pics if he found a horse for me, knowing full well that I didn't have cell service while I was out and about on this island.

So I finished the conversation and went out with my friend for the day. We talked a bit about the horse auction, my friend and I, but I didn't expect anything to happen on that day.

A little side note about this synchronistic story. The week before, I had celebrated my 44th birthday. That same week, I had an astrological reading about 44 because of my birthday. I have always had a big connection to numbers through 11s as you already know, so when I see repetitions, I pay attention.

I returned home at about 4 PM. As soon as I got back on Wi-Fi, I had a text come through. It was from the man at the auction. His message was this: "I have your horse on the truck and we're heading back to our ranch. She is a four-year-old dry mare and has a kind eye . . ."

I read this text out loud and my husband and friend stood in front of me with wide eyes. I quickly sent him back a note saying, "What? I didn't send you any money and approve the purchase of a horse."

He sent back, "Oh ya, it's okay. I can find a home for her if you don't want her. I had a bunch of people and I mixed you in. Anyway, she is in your name if you decide you want her."

Of course I asked him to send a video of her. Well, in the video I see this beautiful sorrel (orange-coloured) mare with a blond mane . . . oh man . . . and then she turns her butt toward the video, and there, painted on her hindquarters, is the number 44!

Well, that was it. Stick a fork in me, I'm done! How can you argue with that kind of synchronicity? This mare was supposed to come to Soulfarm. Most people don't live their lives this way, basing decisions on numbers, knowing it is planned by Source, but hey, I'm not everybody.

I knew that Luna needed to come here, and I knew that she was answering my call for a children's horse, but during our first months together, I definitely had my doubts. Could she be safe with children, was she going to hurt someone? Would she ever be rideable? These questions kept running through me, but as soon as each question arrived, there came a feeling of trust and knowing right behind it.

My trust in my own intuition as my Wild knowing grows through each of these experiences. The coolest really is when I put out a call, and the call is answered, and I have doubt after doubt but I keep my faith . . . and it works out to be aligned in the most specific ways.

My intuition is the only thing that I have come to trust. I feel my deep connection to who I naturally am and to the soul part of myself, and really this connection is the answer to everything we want.

Luna arrives

Luna had to come from Alberta, so it took her a few weeks to make her way here, with many stops along the way. You can imagine that once she got here, even though she was reported to be very sweet, she was pretty tightly wound.

My friend drove the trailer onto the property. We had planned that I would hold the other two horses by their halters and that Luna would be unloaded into the adjacent field (the only place with separate fencing).

The moment they drove onto the property, the horses knew exactly what was going on and the whinnying began. Everyone was very excited! They unloaded Luna, and she proceeded to run across said field and jump the fence to be with us! So much for quarantine! I was holding Raven by her halter because I could see what was about to happen, but Piper was still tied. I had to let go of the rope and halter during the uproar to keep myself safe.

All three horses proceeded to run around the entire property with Piper's ears pinned and teeth bared. I had never seen anything like that in this old guy. Piper was protecting Raven and attacking Luna every time she came near. This carried on through the evening, even though they had moments of calm.

I wanted to separate them again, but I figured Luna would just jump the fence again and we don't have the facilities to really lock them up anywhere to settle down. They would just have to figure it out. I came out at midnight to check on them, and Piper had been kicked in the teeth and was bleeding and hurting. I checked him out, saw that he was okay, and proceeded to get my lawn chair and sleeping bag. It was going to be a long night! They were all eating calmly after a while, so I gave them a loud lecture and went in for the remainder of the short morning.

Journal entry:

It has now been almost five months since Luna arrived. The horses are surprisingly still integrating. There is something really special about this (even though it is driving me crazy!). The reason I find it special is that I know they are pointing out so much to me. I am not so egocentric that I think every little thing my horses do is for me, but I have been around them long enough now to see that when something isn't shifting, there is usually something for me to learn. And when I learn the thing, they shift. It's one more of those can't-believe-it-until-you-experience-it things that happens with horses.

This happened a week ago with Piper and Luna. They have settled a lot, but since she came, Piper has definitely lost his place in the herd, or whatever place he thought he had. Piper and Raven are both very laid back, but it has come clear to me that Piper gets pushy when he is anxious — hence the big blow up when Luna arrived. He also doesn't see well at night, so lately, he has been scared at night of the mares — even Raven.

Because he lost his place and has realized it, they are pushing him off food. It isn't very dramatic for the two of them to jostle, but for him to be jostling in the dark has been getting really dangerous for him and for me. Because he doesn't see well, his anxiety is through the roof, and he seems not to see me when I'm feeding them, so I can't rely on being safe around him.

So one night last week, I got really scared and came to the end of my rope, feeling like I couldn't keep Piper safe, and he shouldn't be running around in the dark hurting himself, and that he needs to be in a stall at night.

I talked to a wise friend on the phone about it and she reflected back to me what I had been feeling from the horses: that this was no big deal, that everything was okay, and that we humans were making a big hairy deal out of nothing. We finished our conversation and got off the phone.

That evening when I went out for the evening feed, and again later to check on them, and the horses were standing quietly around the barn, with no jostling, as if to say, "What exactly is your problem?" And since then, for the last week, life has been pretty blissful around here!

Horse magic

"Become a force of peace in the world." —SADHGURU

It's been years since I moved from the city to a trailer on this island farm. I started with one, two, and now we have three horses, two goats, two dogs, one cat, three kids, hubby, and me.

We are a community of 13, a circle of 13.

We have come together (at least the animals and I) for the purposes of offering a healing sanctuary for people to experience their connection to their own soul. This is guaranteed. Never has someone come here and not felt the peace that emanates from the land and animals.

By co-creating this space for healing, I've had to really put my faith in this "horse magic" that I've experienced and know to be true. It took me a long time to stop tripping over my doubts that nothing was happening in a session with the horses. I could feel the opportunities to shift, and had experienced that working with the horses and asking things of them was teaching us about how to hold our power.

I was also convinced that trust is the medicine of the horse. I could feel that horses hook us up with our own souls and then show us what stands in the way. But what I wasn't fully convinced about was the actual movement and shifting of energy that horses do all the time.

There was still plenty of doubt in me about this "magic" part. I doubted the magic in them just like I doubted the magic in me.

Until I slowly started to feel the magic during a session. At first, I saw a movement or something in the physical body language of a horse and then I knew something about what the horses were wanting to show the person. Then, I started to see and feel things on such a deeper, more subtle level. Now, we just open a space for healing to happen when a person comes for a session and the magic begins.

But things aren't always revealed immediately. A relationship with a horse is like any relationship. You get to know them over time and they reveal one piece of your truth to you at a time, when you're ready, and not before.

They seem to know the limited ability of the human body to hold vibration. Like when I was a child, having big energetic experiences, the mind can shut down quickly if it feels like there's too much, and so can the body. So the horses deliver the medicine gently to me and to those who come to experience it.

Like any true alchemist knows, the universe only gives us what we're ready for, and what we can hold.

This is the same with manifestation. We might be asking for something bigger and bolder, but we can't have that thing until we can hold the vibration of the thing we want.

For example, if I want 11 horses, but I can't currently imagine having 11 horses, I won't be able to have them. Or, if we can't imagine the special love relationship we want, or whatever it is.

That's why we practice as if we're already there and can feel what it's like to have what we want.

So it is with intuitive growth and remembering who we are. If we can imagine what it feels like to be deeply connected to our instinct and intuition, to have our senses open, and to be connected to all that is, receiving and transmitting energy, light and energy, we'll be doing just that!

Part 2:
Feel Your Magic

Magic

I find it so funny in our society that we don't talk about magic. Magic is the word I use for what you might call "Source" or "God." Words are incredibly powerful and have such different meanings for people with different experiences, so let's stick with "magic."

While I see magic as flowing though everyone and everything, when I speak of your "Wild," I am talking about your soul. I see our Wild as our personal Source, the part of us that has been with us and is specifically interested in what we are doing. Our Wild carries us through life as we follow our purpose, with our specific likes, dislikes, and passions.

I believe that if we follow our Wild, we will be brought to our purpose here in this life. I believe that we are here on earth to allow our passion to lead us to create our manifestation , and I know that when we do this, it creates a vibration that is healing the earth. When many of us get on this path, well, everything changes.

I know that you have felt the power of your Wild, and have had nudges from it in your life. Maybe you are someone who follows the Wild in you no matter what. But maybe, you're like I was. You know that there is magic running through everything, but you have such heavy conditioning that you have to push and fight and struggle against yourself and the people around you to follow your Wild.

I've always known that everything is vibrational and that the path to knowing our Wild is through the body. We find the truth of us within our bodies and within our energy centres. Many wisdom traditions speak of these places in the body where energy pools in wheels or "chakras." They discuss how these vibrational centres connect into both our bodies and our endocrine systems. They also teach how these energetic centres each connect into a different level of consciousness.

The horses know this. If you watch the horses over many years, and connect with them intuitively, you will start to see how their work is to balance each other and us. You will see them balance each other by touching their own bodies and each other. Sometimes they will roll, which grounds the horse and those around him/her. They will also hold space for us to get our act together.

Anyone who has spent time with horses knows that they mirror back to us, but this mirroring isn't always physical. Mostly it is energetic. So often the horses will be mirroring something back to me on a subtle level that I can't quite put my finger on, but I can feel it in the air. I can feel it hovering between us. On a basic intuitive level, they are showing us something about ourselves.

I used to think that this mirroring would happen only on the physical level, and that I needed to watch closely how the horses "acted" when someone was with us, but by experience and by paying close attention, I realized that they are subtle beings, and so I had to become very subtle too, to translate for my clients. I can see the horses from my windows every day, so I spend a lot of time watching and understanding them.

At first I was skeptical. When I trained in this specific healing work, I was thinking, "Ya right, there's nothing happening; they're just eating grass. Sure it's cool to be around them because they're big, but nothing is really happening."

But as things go with me, I followed what felt good, and so I found myself back with the horses again and again. I started accepting that maybe nothing was happening, but it felt damn good to be around the horses anyway, and each time I left feeling changed and wanting more. Then I had a few spiritual experiences with them. And then, of course, I wanted something big and wonderful to happen each time I was with them!

My Gemini expectations of "wow" and "aha" moments went off the charts, and I began to feel disappointed if I didn't have a big download or an amazing experience when I was with the horses.

But then, I started to notice how subtle they are. I started to feel into our regular sessions where I didn't get big explosive "ahas" or feel big shifts in my body, and I discovered that these hangouts had just as much shifting going on — it was just more subtle.

How the horses walk with us through the energy centres

In this next section, I'll show you how the horses took me through the energy centres and helped me to heal all the vibrational levels of myself so that I can be living from my Wild.

I must insert here that much of my work is through "vision journeys" and "soul readings." I will speak of this more in the third eye section, but I have always had the ability to receive information from Source. I didn't call it channeling or even know what it was. I used to be terrified of it, actually, which I'll discuss more later. My intuition would show up in different ways, sometimes scaring me and often confusing me.

But as I practiced and became more focused (and as Raven started partnering with me), I have been using the vision journey process in my work with others and always with myself. I will share many of these journeys with you in the next part of the book, as well as physical experiences that the horses have brought to me for my healing.

I see it like this: The horses that do this work come to help us on our journey back to our Wild. They partner with us and walk with us. I have seen it time and time again with myself and with my clients. The horses are here as our biggest supporters, even when we don't see what is happening (which, honestly, is most of the time).

Being highly sensitive

"Some days I am more wolf than woman and I am still learning how to stop apologizing for my wild."

—NIKITA GILL

I am highly sensitive. Always have been. I'm guessing you are too. I'm guessing you feel big and sense big. I'm guessing you had many places in your life where you wanted to create and let your mind run free while society told you that you must do "sensible" things. Or that you were told you needed to "suck it up" when you were feeling something in a big way.

Those of us who are highly sensitive learn to be pretty good at hiding ourselves. We learn to hold a tight cloak around us as protection.

We take all that too-muchness and sensitivity and hide it away in our shadow. This is where we first learn the art of control. To feel acceptable in this world, we have to control ourselves, but "controlling ourselves" can become an addiction.

Linda Kohanov talks about this in her "Way of the Horse" cards. In card 26, Promise, she says, "A soul trained into submission cannot truly experience joy, cannot truly express love."

This collective anxiety then leads to the world setting up restrictions in hopes of keeping us safe, but all this control we have put on ourselves and on society is actually making us sicker.

I know this because I lived this way for so long. This living in fear actually causes us to separate ourselves from the world, physically, emotionally, and energetically.

The only thing that actually heals us is connection, and feeling our inner power and worth! We can have everything else, but without connection, we will wither and break. This is starting to be seen in the world with divorce levels increasing, depression and anxiety statistics, and suicide levels increasing.

"Wild is the soul where passion and creativity reside,
and the quickening of your heart.
Wild is what is real, and wild is your home."

—VICTORIA ERICKSON

Horses and sensitivity

In the horse world, you will often hear people say, "Horses aren't sensitive. You don't have to feel bad using a rope to whack them to move forward. Look how big they are! It's like me doing this to you," as they touch you lightly on the hand.

This doesn't sit well with me. My knowing overrides all of it. First, if you watch a horse, you will see how very sensitive they are. They can feel a fly landing on their skin. They can feel an emotion hidden deep inside of you. They can feel everything.

Those of us who are naturally extremely sensitive understand this. We feel everything that other people feel. All of our senses are intense. This can make our world beautiful and we can be full of awe, breathing and seeing and hearing and sensing and feeling beauty — and we can be fully feeling all of the darkness around us.

We can feel the fear of an incident that is happening thousands of miles away. We can sense the emotion of every single person that walks through the door — and we have to discern where all of this is coming from. When it's beautiful, it's lovely to bask in the beauty of the world, but when it's not beautiful, it hurts.

And so we learn, through experiences and through watching the horses, how to feel everything, but to not to let it all into our energetic systems. A huge part of this is learning to be present, because if we are not present, all of this information overload causes a vibration of anxiety within us.

Horses teach us to be fiercely present in all moments in all that we do. This fierce presence is the antidote to anxiety. If we are fully in the moment, experiencing it with all of our senses, we are unable to feel anxious. We may feel the symptoms, still, of a racing heart and dizziness, but the racing thoughts will lessen (because you can't have thoughts when you are fully in the moment, using all of your senses).

In the next chapters, we will see a myriad of ways that horses are brilliant teachers in Supersensing 101.

But first . . . a secret!

For us to really and truly heal, we have to give up "the story." All of what you have already read is my story. It's a huge part of who I have become and also a huge part of what I rely on. Every morning, when I wake out of my bliss, I search around myself for something in "reality" to ground myself, and my story is my touchstone. It is what, in an instant, brings back all of who I think I am in this moment. But when we really decide to heal, we are asked to give up this story.

I was asked this one morning recently as I had been dealing for days with an old pain in my shoulder. The pain was big, had been going on for days, and had been threatening to take over my whole back and seize up like it used to when I really needed to listen to my soul.

So I sat with this pain, deep in hypnosis and in meditation. This came to me:

"You cannot heal unless you stop telling that old, boring story."

When I looked deeply into these subtle feelings, under my frustration, inside this pain that has been such a big part of my life, I could see that this story was serving me somehow.

When I really sit with it, I can detect a fleeting feeling under this pain. I would venture to say that you might have this feeling too, about the main situation in your life that you are having trouble shifting, be it success in health, abundance, relationships, or whatever it is. The feeling is that of the victim.

This victim feeling in me is something I picked up somewhere along my trail and this belief must have worked for me at some point: If I am weak physically, I get attention. Ooofff. That one is hard to admit and sit with.

It's hard to see it in writing, that I could actually have this belief. But I stand by it. If I look back, as a child looking for attention and support (like we all are), I sure got a lot of attention and support by being sick.

It took years of my parents' attention to help me with my gut issues, taking me to this doctor and that, and my mom cooking me all kinds of special meals. I'm not saying I did this in a manipulative way, because I certainly would have given up years of feeling sick for less of that kind of attention, but I can feel it festering underneath it all. And so, I have to be willing to give up this story to really heal. And I am.

I am ready to be solid and confident and to take up space in my body on this earth. I am ready for that.

All it takes to heal is a commitment. Making a decision is the most powerful thing you can do in your healing. I decide to be me without this story. I decide to be the me that is beyond all of this pain and joy that I have lived already. I decide to be Me, who is new every single day.

Connection heals

Connection doesn't have to be with other humans only, but we have to find connection with something. Nature heals us. We would never see animals living disconnected from each other or from the earth, because that would mean death for them. Their connection to nature and to each other is their lifeline.

I can't explain this "something is off" feeling that I have had for so long. It is at its roots a distrust, a first energy centre feeling of being unsafe on this planet. I know I'm not the only one feeling this.

There are so many of us who feel like aliens here on this earth. We are the ones with past life work to heal for ourselves and our lineage. We are the ones who were not accepted for who we are, and might have suffered dire consequences for it. Maybe our ancestors did as well. We carry the energy of that pain, hurt, and even terror and chaos into this life. We don't always know it's there, following us around and keeping us unable to live freely and happily.

This is my purpose in this lifetime, to help people release these things they are carrying. To help them feel the power of who they are so that they can shine that out to the world, and in turn, heal the world. The horses are showing up to work with me in this powerful endeavour. The years we have spent together so far have been to the end of healing others, but also, they have helped me to heal myself!

The horses know that the only way for us to heal and to become fully integrated, powerful human beings, is to reconnect with our Wild selves.

Soulfarm

Because I was so obsessed with controlling my world to keep myself safe, I made myself sick. This is an easy thing to see from a higher perspective, but letting go of control day to day when one has built a life on it is a difficult venture indeed.

Just as I committed to following my soul to the life she wanted for me after my divorce, I committed to healing my body when we moved to the farm.

I had been told by a psychic after getting this property that as I relaxed and sank into the earth, all of my physical difficulties would disappear.

So when we named our new farm "Soulfarm," and I created Soulfarm Healing Company, I knew this would be my path to healing. I trusted that setting this as an intentional healing place, and commitment to that vision, would create a magic space for people to find connection to who they are, and for healing to take place.

The horses became obvious co-workers for me. I say that horses hook you up with your soul self and show you what's standing in the way energetically of this soul connection being solid, and then they help you heal that. This work is basically a path to enlightenment and freedom. I say "a" path because there are so many, but this is a powerful one!

The horses point us to our Wild

"A finger pointing at the moon is not the moon. The finger is needed to know where to look for the moon, but if you mistake the finger for the moon itself, you will never know the real moon."

—THICH NHAT HANH

To me, the horses are the finger. They are pointing us toward our Wild. They are not going to scream and stamp and yell to us about what we aren't seeing in ourselves and who we really are at a soul level. They aren't going to pick us up on their backs and deliver us to a place where we are physically standing in front of our truth, but if we sit with them as a practice and become open to their teachings, they will lead us to our souls every single time.

The energetics

During my training as a Equine Facilitated Wellness practitioner, I wrote this poem. The horses live on a different level of consciousness than we do in our regular daily lives. I have committed to spend as much time in that space as possible, which is why I now spend my life with three horses. I didn't know why I was choosing this change in my life. I was just following my heart that led me here.

This space, where the horses live, is an energetic space. They see us as energetic beings. This poem about the energy centres, or chakras, was inspired by the horses.

Root Chakra

Love the earth
I am the energy of connectedness
I am the energy of the physicality of the Human
I am the Earth
She is me
I am her
Stability. I support myself
Security. I am safe.
Being. I am here now.
I am this moment and I am connected to all that is
and to myself and to the Earth.

Sacral Chakra

Loves creating and loves feeling deeply into LIfe.
She embodies relationships with the other
Honour Self, Honour the Other.
Create from the depths of the water.
Dive into the feelings and create from their energy.
The energy of creation.
The energy of sex.
The energy of the swirl of masculine and feminine.
Be and Do. Do and Be.
Be do be do be do be.
Joy in the creation.
I love creating! Let's create!

Solar plexus Chakra

The Self and the Sun
The Plexus of the Self
The Centre where the Self grows and becomes
The Self exudes warmth and confidence
Self is Sun is Solar
Solar energy, Self energy
When I believe in mySelf, I am energized for Life
I know where I end and you begin
I know what feels good for my Soul
I feel the nuances of Life here
I shine my Soul
My Soul shines Me

Heart Chakra

LOVE, from within
Comes from the deep
Explodes out of us
Not connected to anything
Just is.
Love,
Green and healing
Ready for action
Just waiting
For a request
Stationed at the ready
Wanting healing
Wanting alignment
Love is the natural state of everything

Love,
Awe and compassion
The human is Sacred
The animals are here
For our connection take place within ourselves
Love.

High heart Chakra

Pink. Turquoise. Tortoise.
Peace lives here
All beings join together and shine pink
Humans hold hands with light beings
White and red make pink.
Join energy, join light.
Be the love that we shine.
The love that joins in peace
Runs through every river of life.
All beings feel the call
We lift our eyes from the show
And we rise.
Peace.

Throat Chakra

The sky speaks its blue story
Through this space in time.
Open to the will from above
And let life move you to its rhythm.
Truth. Speak. Express.
Feelings bubble to this place from below
Explore and release.
A song of life is written here
And truth soars above the mountains.

Third eye Chakra

Everything knows and is knowns Universe inside
Expansion. Connected.
See beyond curtains.
Sleep, awake, vortex
Eyes see symbols and metaphors
Truths in images.
Beyond.

Crown Chakra

The queen wears a crown
Light shines filling it from above
Violet petals of the lotus
Connected to Angels
Sparkles dance in the rainbow within
Fairies giggle through whirlpools
I am everything
Bliss.

—THIRZA VOYSEY

Join me on the energetic journey through the energy centres that the horses took me through and find ways to balance and cleanse your own energy centres!

Part 3: Be Your Wild 1st Energy Centre/ Root Chakra

1st Energy Centre
Root Chakra

The moon is full above the brightly burning fire in the centre of the labyrinth. It is the 20th of September, the Equinox. My eyes are closed as the shamanic drumming thunders through my centre. I feel connected to everything in the night — the moon, the fire, the people sitting beside me, and the horses. As I drift in my reverie, I see the black horse in my mind's eye. The horse rises up, flying toward the moon, up the sides of the caduceus, the symbol for healing, with the snake winding up. As I watch the horse fly up with her magical dark wings, I see the moon radiating from behind her.

My third eye is throbbing with this vision and I have goose flesh all over. I come back to myself while holding this beautiful image in my mind, and I breathe deeply, noticing the drumming again. I feel my body sitting in the chair, I feel the breath in my lungs, I feel the cold night air on my face, and then the thundering starts. I feel it first, then I hear it, then quickly a knowing runs through me. The horses are running. They gallop around the outside of the circle in the darkness. I feel the Wildness in me rising up as I sit, cozy in my seat, with my blanket wrapped around me. I am not afraid. I feel bliss.

The drumming eventually stops and I slowly get up to leave the circle and follow the others outside the labyrinth, back to the house for apple cider. I stand and as I do, I feel a powerful knowing within me that I will see the black horse. Spirit is the name of the black horse in this herd. He is the wise herd leader and has been training me over the better part of a year to be a medicine horse facilitator. Since our first meeting, I have felt a strong draw between the two of us and our recognition of each other.

I know this wise beast has so much to teach me. As I walk out of the labyrinth and focus on where I am putting my feet in the darkness, I catch a glimpse of something. Sure enough, when I lift my head, I see Spirit, just outside the labyrinth, grazing in the cool light of the full moon. I walk up to him and feel his warm breath on my cold hands. Spirit is the most grounded being I have ever met, and I feel as if I want to curl up next to him and sleep, or live within his amazing energy. I can't put my finger on the feeling, but when I am next to this great being, I finally feel safe. The coziness of being next to this beast is like a sleeping pill, and I suddenly feel very much like snuggling up. Picturing the owner coming out in the morning to find me sleepy-eyed in the barn, I think better of it and head to the house for a cup of apple cider, and then home.

The first energy centre, also called the root chakra, or muladhara in Sanskrit, involves the level of consciousness of your family of origin, your physical body, where you live, your belief systems, trust and fear, and feeling supported financially and emotionally. The Wild in this centre forms during the first seven years of life as we learn what it is like to be here on earth.

So much of what you experience in these first years creates the energies in this centre.

This is why, during work with the horses, we do a lot of inner child work. Healing our bodies and minds is so dependent on a healthy first energy centre, so we go back in visualizations and meet and talk to the inner child. These meetings transform the energies of this centre immensely.

The Wild here smells like deep earth, it feels like the ground under you; its colour is a clear, bright red. The energy here feels solid, grounded, and calm. It feels connected to the earth, heavy, and safe. It feels so good and soothing to be grounded in this way. I watch the horses ground themselves and release old energies by rolling on the ground, and it looks like it feels so good.

The first chakra is the place where we dump all of the old beliefs and toxins out of our bodies and energetic systems. It's important for us to do regular energetic clearing so that we can use this space for its intended purpose, to keep us safe, keep us calm, and for manifesting our dreams into the physical world.

If this chakra isn't clear, it is impossible for us to bring our dreams into reality through this centre. Basically, we release toxins into the earth both through bodily functions and through energetically grounding. If our root chakra is blocked because of a lack of grounding or belief systems that keep us from feeling safe in the world, our body is unable to detoxify itself, and that extra energy can get trapped in the root and sacral chakras, leaving us feeling overly emotional and anxious.

And so with the horses, I work with people by walking them through this centre. What is showing up in my world is a mirror for me, and I am also healed by each of these experiences.

"There's no greater way to connect back with the wild Soul than by returning to our most ancient roots."

—TARA ISIS, WILD WOMAN SISTERHOOD

Horses who are calm and happy have grounding figured out. When left alone by humans, they graze, meditate, and rest, moving around slowly, with bursts of play and rambunctiousness. If something scares them, they quickly move away or do what needs to be done to become safe again and then they go back to chilling out. They have four feet on the ground and big bodies that hold them very solidly in the world.

Piper, right now, is lying on the grass in our front yard, just chilling out, with Raven watching over him.

Their natural way of grounding is to roll on the ground. It makes sense; they get many benefits from rolling, including massage, an acupressure treatment, and connection with the earth over their whole body.

I have watched our horses over the time they've been with us, and have observed them settle into the space, literally. When Raven first came to live with us, she didn't lie down for probably the first six months. Then one day, I came upon her and her horse friend lying down one at a time in the forested area. Horses often will arrange themselves with one as the guard while the other lies down. Never have I seen them roll consecutively together, until one day when a client came for a session.

Remember that horses are interested in balancing the energetics of anyone who comes, but often they do this without touching the human. Since we are all connected, they will balance the energy on their own bodies or on each other.

The woman arrived, telling me that she was feeling really ungrounded and emotional after a conflictual phone call. She left it at that, not wanting to dwell on the details, and we switched our attention to the horses. She was afraid to go inside the fence, so we calmly stood by the gate. The horses both came up to say hi, and then they started to roll, one after the other. One would roll, and then immediately the other would come in and roll in the exact same spot.

The horses were clearly saying, “This is your message! You need to ground yourself! Your energy is all over the place and this is what we do when that happens. It helps. Wanna join?” Ha ha. I didn’t hear them talking, but it was a very clear message. Especially since as soon as they were finished rolling, they walked away from us and ate grass, as if to say, “That’s the message for today’s session and now we’re done.” I was surprised that it was so simple and to the point for this client, but she felt the message powerfully. We did some more work together after that, but she expressed that she had received the message loud and clear from these beings and was feeling better already. We did more grounding work and then she went home and did more on her own.

Having grounding techniques in our bag of tricks is more than essential. It is a necessity of life. That is not to say that you have to get off your chair at work and start rolling around in the middle of the hall after a stressful meeting (although at times that would feel so great!). It does, however, mean that you go back to your desk, feel your feet where they connect to your shoes and the earth, and do some deep breaths with the intention of connecting yourself with the earth. Even better, go outside and sit by a tree or a rock or right on the ground. Take your shoes and socks off if you can and get some of that good soil between your toes.

Grounding, or "earthing," as some call it, has been getting much attention lately for its healing benefits. In the documentary film, "Grounded," a man decides to go and live in Alaska by himself where he creates a grounding experience for people who have health issues. He includes earthing, as many health benefits come from being in connection with the earth. There is also a book called Earthing: The Most Important Health Discovery Ever! In it, the authors speak of the importance of connecting our bodies to the earth physically. They say that the process of absorbing earth's free flowing electrons from its surface through the soles of one's feet heals us.

Recently, I felt this connection to the energy of the earth in a visceral way. I had a lot of lower back pain after two pretty major car accidents in my early 20s (they were two weeks apart — how's that for a big message?). I was always a runner, and even after the accidents, I would run regularly. I had intense sciatic pain, but running was what I knew and it felt good, so that's what I did.

I started to accept that back pain had something to do with feeling unsupported (at that time I didn't accept the energetic aspect of healing, but I was looking at the emotional reasons). Because I realized I didn't feel supported in many ways, I used to imagine sitting on the earth, my butt right there up in the air with the whole globe underneath me. It was a funny visual but it was powerful for me, and even though I didn't realize at the time, it really was about the earth supporting me energetically like she supports all her creatures.

I was watching the horses with this in mind. They just walk around and do their thing, but you can tell how much they trust that they will get another meal from Mother Earth and that she will continue to be there for them to graze on and relax on. They really are very trusting of this and you can almost see the energy from the earth running up their big legs into their bodies. In fact, the way they saunter across the earth reveals them as incredibly grounded beings.

So one day, I had fed the animals and was sitting on the ground after meditating, with the morning sun warming me. I love to do this because it makes me feel like I'm hanging with the herd. On this particular day, I felt the energy of the earth rushing into my root chakra (at the base of my trunk, at the perineum). I had been practicing a meditation where I drop my grounding cord, or imaginary straw, down into the core of the earth and suck up all the crystalline energy from the centre of the Mother into my body. I did this on that day and something dawned on me: energetically, we are often not connecting with the earth. We are so busy trying to control our lives and avoid things that scare us in order to feel some semblance of safety and support, that we are blocking the true support from the earth.

In a being with a balanced root chakra, light energy comes in and toxic, old stuff gets released into the earth. The earth then transforms this toxic sludge back into light energy, which we can draw up into ourselves at any time. If, like the animals, we could remain grounded at all times, we would feel supported in all ways by the earth at all times. We wouldn't need to fly off the handle in fear about anything, not money, not bills, not where we're going to live, or what job to take, or any of it.

Having a balanced first energy centre means that you have a deep trust in the earth. This is the important work that the horses and I are doing. Together, we are helping people reconnect with those Wild parts of themselves, with their power, by connecting to the earth and her beings. By seeing the sacredness in the natural world, we are able to see the sacredness in ourselves.

We really need to have a balanced root chakra in order to work in this magical way. This is the work of so many indigenous peoples. We in the westernized world are finally starting to realize that without that deep, honouring connection with the earth, we cannot live our empowered, healthy lives. This is the grave importance of the first energy centre, connection to the earth.

Having this grounding piece figured out with the help of the horses also really assists in our abilities to manifest our life. The lower three chakras, the earth chakras, are the manifestors extraordinaire. Without them, ideas would abound, but would never get manifested.

It works like this: the upper chakras, or more refined energies, come up with the grand ideas and dreams, through thinking and visualizing. Then, the idea drops down into the heart, we feel it there, and see if our heart approves. If it's a big ole yes, the energy of this creation drops down into the lower three chakras and gets manifested into the world in physical form, much like a baby does. There is a physicality that is required for ideas to become things.

Grounding with an anxious horse

I really felt the power of the earth in me recently. We went to visit a horse who was extremely anxious, to see about bringing her to Soulfarm. I could feel her vibrating from the first moment I saw her. She was a ball of nerves and fear. I could feel it rising in myself, but I went to her. I continually reminded myself to be in my body and stay grounded by being aware of my feet. Her vibration was still apparent and I felt it, but I didn't let it take over (I can sometimes get so overwhelmed by the energy that I start to vibrate physically).

I knew that I had the skills to connect with this horse and work with her. I became quiet and came into her energetic bubble with her. I forgot about all the other people there (my husband and kids and the two owners) and connected, just the horse and me. I knew instantly that my heart needed to be open. She is an incredibly open mare with a huge heart. So I focused on opening my heart and then we started to work together. I wanted to show her that I understood and accepted her and that I could connect with her on her level.

I used my horse connection skills to find out how sensitive she was. While I was leading her around, she was able to go and stop when I used only "thought" and "energy" for cues. Often horses will need you to start louder, with words and gestures to understand you, but not this girl. She was sensitive and it was beautiful. I could tell, though, that she had had a very difficult time in life. She had an incredibly traumatic past, and trust was her issue. I decided that if I could work with this horse, I would work on only the root chakra.

Unfortunately, I wasn't able to bring this mare home with us. For many reasons, she wasn't meant to be with us at that time, but with help from her people and a trusted trainer who has the horse's needs at the front of mind and heart, she has since made leaps and bounds in her healing. I know that they've been helping her with her root chakra.

During this experience with the anxious mare, I felt my own connection with my roots. I could feel the support of the energy of the earth rushing through me, calming my mind, and allowing me to do the work that I know. Without that calm, I would have reacted from fear, and possibly anger (which I used to do when my horse got anxious, because it made me afraid).

Trust

Learning to trust came next on the journey.

Trust is a big one for us humans. It can rear its head in relation to abundance and trusting that money will keep coming to support our dreams, and it comes up during health issues.

Worrying is a flat out lack of trust in the universe. The root chakra is the place where we feel secure on the earth, trust that the earth will continue to nurture us, and that our bodies will keep us healthy. As we have lost much of our connection to the earth, we have dissolved much of this trust we had as infants. We came to the planet knowing that our every need would be taken care of. It is not until this trust is broken by life experiences that we lose it. Our work now is to regain this connection with our inherent trust.

Much of the work to reconnect with our trust of life, the earth, and our bodies is done through a reconnection with nature. Through this work, essentially finding our Wild selves again, we can connect back in with our natural instincts and our intuition. When we trust, life flows. But to know that life will always be there for us, we have to feel deserving and worthy of this constant abundance. The horses show us this because they know their worth.

Having the experience of working with a 1200-pound being that could bolt at any moment, running you over, makes you reach for something beyond yourself for sure. Trust has to be built. Building trust between a human and a horse is one of the most beautiful things I have ever witnessed.

In that moment when a person or a horse softens into trust, it makes me bawl every time with joy. And it usually comes with tears on the part of the client too. This release of the way we hold ourselves tight and in control is a full time job for most of us. It leaves our bodies tight and rigid, usually with pain and other difficulties. But the reason I love it when I see trust being built between horse and human is because I know that as soon as the person begins to trust the horse, they are learning to trust themselves as well.

I Belong

I belong on the Earth.
My magnificence is called forth.

As I was being adopted into the herd,
I could feel something there that the horses were pointing out,
But I couldn't see it clearly.

It was the belief that I don't belong.
They were opening the door, but my belief
Which became a wall kept me out.

Until it came crumbling down.
The pain to stay separate from the
Huge love that the horses had for
Me became more than the pain
Of letting go of that old belief.

I let go of this separateness,
I feel held
I feel welcomed and warm.

The ground under me no longer feels
Shaky or unsteady.
It feels sure.
I belong.

After this session with the herd,
I no longer feel like I am running toward something.
That sense of competition that there are only a few spots . . .
Instead I feel like I have fallen into a cosy nest where
everything that I enjoy is there for me,
A place where my creativity within feels playful.

I feel the vastness of time.
I feel the depth of my presence.

I Belong.
Thank you.

—THIRZA VOYSEY

Fierce presence

"The Divine lives inside this place. Not in our minds, not in our ideas that we are god, but inside this presence that is who we are, what beats our hearts and channels our truth into service and art and being and connection." —SACRED_ALCHEMY (INSTAGRAM).

Be in the present moment. The body is the key to being present. Humans are craving peace of mind. The body is already present. It is here now. If we put attention on the body, we'll find that a still body equals a still mind.

The horses teach us incredibly well about the importance of being in our body. The industry calls it "somatic," meaning "of the body." A somatic therapy session in a therapist's office would be very different from a session with a horse. With the former, the client or patient would sit and experience the trauma while the therapist watches to see how the body experiences the trauma. This would then be dealt with in a myriad of ways. With the horses, they teach us how to be in our bodies in a powerful way, and then from this powerful place, we can look back over our traumas, which don't feel as powerful when we are fully in our bodies.

In a herd, it is necessary that a horse is in its body, otherwise it can be dangerous for the herd. When not in our bodies, we are not in the present moment, and could end up being a perfect lunch for a predator. Much like humans, horses will disassociate from their experiences, being "out of their bodies." This looks different in different animals, but I generally experience this as a horse being "out of their eyes." It's like there is no energy in their eyes anymore. I had this experience with Raven and a client that came to the farm.

The woman was out in the field with Raven and I. Raven was eating grass beside us, and the woman was chatting about her life. She started to float away on her story and get really caught up with what was going on in it. I asked her to come back to petting Raven and the moment. As she tried to do this, Raven looked up quickly, stepped on the woman's foot, and ran off after the goats. Like with many session experiences, I haven't seen Raven act like this before or since.

I thought that my client might be really hurt or angry, but she immediately got the message and was grateful to Raven for bringing her back into her body. She was able to see the big mirror reflecting her disassociation from her own life.

The horses teach people this intense state of presence when they come for sessions, and the clients can take that feeling of being fully in their bodies into the world with them. Once people experience this state of fierce presence for themselves, the transformation is palpable.

A young woman came to the farm. She had been here before for work with the horses as part of a group. I could see the power within this girl, but she wasn't feeling it within herself. I showed her how to lead Raven with her intention instead of with the lead rope. She stood at Raven's shoulder and asked her to walk. Raven ignored her. I had confidence that Raven could do this, so I knew we could carry on with the teaching. The issue was whether the client could be in the present moment, or whether she would stay in her head.

I asked her to connect up with her own soul and then to connect her heart to Raven's heart. As soon as she asked her to walk this time, Raven lifted her head like she had heard her and walked right along beside her. The girl looked at me with disbelief in her eyes at what had happened. "It's like magic," she said. It really was.

"To stay present in everyday life, it helps to be deeply rooted within yourself; otherwise, the mind, which has incredible momentum, will drag you along like a wild river." —ECKHART TOLLE

A while ago, I was on a walk, feeling really sorry for myself. I had been having a sore belly day and was frustrated because of it. I went for a walk like I always do, stating, "I am going to walk until I have an answer or until I feel better." As I walked, I passed a group of cedar trees under which I often meditate. I followed my heart and the draw to sit there on this day. I leaned against a large cedar and asked for help with this feeling of frustration.

After a few minutes of clearing my mind and listening to the sounds of the forest, an intense feeling came over me. It felt like a deep connection to my body. It felt like my awareness dropped into my body, deeper than it ever had. Used to living up near my mind, I was unfamiliar with this deep feeling of presence. Sure I have experienced it in deep meditation or hypnosis, but the feeling was staying with me in a light state of being. I loved it!

I got up and resumed my hike, carrying this feeling of connection to my body and my life in a new way. I know that I have carried so much fear in my body for so long, that I haven't been fully connected to the moment. Like so many of us, my mind has been so busy with fear and worry that I haven't had the capacity or the space to just be — even though I have sure wanted it!

During this walk, I felt a deep commitment to the present. I felt a commitment to feeling everything emotionally (something we don't do when we disassociate), feeling everything physically (something we don't want to do when we have had a lot of pain in our bodies), and a commitment to experience everything as it comes to me. I know that if I didn't have the horses in my life, teaching me this intense presence daily, I wouldn't have gotten to this place of being in my body.

Raven the Queen

Raven embodies the first three energy centres. She knows her worth. She leads her herd with honour, integrity, and peacefulness, but she is so subtle in her leadership that someone looking on wouldn't know she is leading because she is so subtle. She knows she is the Queen and she trusts that everything will come to her as it should. She doesn't spend time worrying that Mother Earth won't be there to support her feet tomorrow or that there will be no water to drink. She doesn't worry that there will be no hay or pasture tomorrow (she knows that her humans know she is the Queen and will therefore always provide). She knows that she is deserving of such treatment and that those around her will deliver.

This is her biggest work. When others come to be with her, she shows them how to be in their bodies. She shows them that they are worthy of taking up space and that if they don't, they will get bowled over by life (she doesn't actually walk over people, but she does show them how to have great boundaries and how to assert them). She also has a no bullshit attitude. She isn't trying to please a single person. She is being her in all her bigness. She is rocking her 1200 pounds and not asking for permission. She literally sashays, somewhat like a tango dancer, but way bigger and not quite as graceful! But she sure is powerful. Which brings us to the second energy centre or the sacral chakra, the home of our Divine Feminine.

Suggestions from the horses for balancing and cleansing the 1st energy centre:

1. Lie or sit on the ground.
2. Roll around sometimes.
3. Walk barefoot.
4. Be in the present moment when out in nature and as often as you can in life.
5. Look at old belief systems that you are still living by and put them in the fire.
6. Write on a paper what you are letting go of and put it in the fire.
7. Ask spirit to help you release anything that is not for your highest path.
8. Honour your body, bless your food, and feel gratitude at meal times.
9. Go back and visit your young self in meditation and reassure little You that you are safe.
10. Be with horses. Listen. Be.
11. Practice more being and less doing.

Journaling questions:

- Do I feel safe?
- Do I feel connected to my physical body?
- What beliefs and traditions work for me, and which ones am I wanting to let go of?
- Am I connected with nature?
- Do I nurture myself with healthy food, thoughts, and ideas?
- Affirmation for 1st energy centre: I am safe.

2nd Energy Centre/ Sacral Chakra

2nd Energy Centre
Sacral Chakra

"Inside of you is a Wild Woman. Remember her."

—WILD WOMAN SISTERHOOD

The second energy centre, located just below the navel, is one of my favourites. The Wild here sees walls decorated with bright orange flowers, feels the powerful pulsating of the womb, smells vanilla, and hears soft, sexy music playing. The Wild here feels deeply and intensely, while being open and vulnerable in relationships. The feminine and masculine energies are intertwined and balanced here, making the Wild in the flow and also structured in a form that can be shared with the world. This is where we feel our worthiness or lack thereof.

Knowing we are worthy is very much connected to the work of trust which we built in the 1st energy centre. When we feel that we can trust the world and that we are safe in it, we can relax and feel our wellbeing, creativity, and passion, bubble up within us. When we doubt our worthiness, it can show up in our relationships, in our aliveness, in our creativity, in our sexuality, and in our health.

Our creativity and our sexuality, which are so closely connected to each other, live in and are energized by this centre. Because this centre holds so much of our life force energy, if we are drained of energy or feeling lifeless or powerless, it speaks to a loss of power in this centre. This is said to be one of the lowest functioning centres as a whole in our western society.

It's easy to see this when we look at how women are treated, how the feminine energy has been in the background while the masculine has risen, and how creativity isn't seen as sacred in our society. The "Me Too" movement speaks to how many people have been harmed in the second energy centre and have resulting trauma because of it. I believe that each of us has some trauma in this area that the horses can help us work through.

We all have a story of giving up our power. You know my story of feeling connected and powerful at the age of six, and then giving that up to fit in with society. I essentially exchanged my power for a sense of belonging. This is the story for most of us. And it's why we're here — to find and tap into that power again, bringing who we really are to the world through our creativity.

Shame is such a huge contributor to the dark energy that lives in this centre. Shame for being our powerful selves, shame for being "too loud," "too emotional," "too sensitive," or just for being "too much." I would venture to say we all know this story.

This is also the place where our emotions live. It's rare to have grown up in western society in the last few decades and be wonderful at expressing your emotions. I can see our own children being much more clear and to the point and expressive of their emotions than our generation was. I don't know about you, but for me, my biggest goal was to keep everything inside so that first, no one would have to deal with my emotions and feel bad themselves, and second, that no one would see that I wasn't perfect.

The horses want to show us our power within and how very essential it is that we express who we are to the world. This is our magic.

Emotional congruence

"She is a wild, tangled forest with temples and treasures concealed within." —JOHN MARK GREEN

Emotional congruence is essential if you want to be part of a herd. If you aren't acknowledging how you feel, horses will feel threatened or they won't like your unclear energy. Horses' emotions are clear, and they don't seem to do the hiding and stuffing and living in illusion about their emotions that humans do. Horses do, however, have ways of dealing with each other when they are behaving weirdly in a way that doesn't benefit the herd.

They have patterns and roles within the herd that allow them to "work" within a community. If one of the horses in the herd is exhibiting anxious behaviour which is affecting others, one of the horses will walk with him and push him outside of the herd while he calms himself. Then, once the anxious horse is visibly calmer, the herd mate will let him back in the herd and they'll all go back to grazing. As a grounding technique, this is brilliant. It is the horse equivalent of taking space to cool off.

Living the slow life

We live in a very fast world. Anxiety doesn't do well with fast. Moving quickly in mind and body is incredibly ungrounding. Screens and endless access to information make our minds busier and more stressed, while what we need most is just the opposite. An anxious mind needs a slow life.

I knew this on some level when I moved to the farm. I moved from a city, albeit a small city, to a farm on a small island. These decisions, put together, have added up to a slow life. Sure, there are sacrifices that need to be made, but there are so many reasons why this is exactly what I and the other members of my family most needed. And so here we are, living slowness and calmness. Don't get me wrong, we still have Wi-Fi, so life outside still exists, but the feelings of being in the middle of the buzz are not there anymore. And looking out the window to see the animals grazing in the front yard just allows us to breathe deeper and fuller.

I remember seeing a psychic for fun as we were planning to move here, and asking her about my health issues. This is what she said about that: "Once you move, you will become so relaxed that everything will just relax in you and your body will heal."

And well ain't that just what's happening?!

Another thing about slowing down and having patience is going with the flow. Healthy horses are very able to go with the flow. Sure, they like routine, and they have their individual things that they might like or balk at, depending on their upbringing and any traumas they've experienced, but overall, horses can experience something new and if it doesn't hurt them, the next time they are exposed to that thing, they are fine with it.

The energy of the sacral chakra is this energy of going with the flow. It is in the going with the flow that we find joy and bliss. Joy comes from being able to detach ourselves from the "what ifs" of life. *Abraham-Hicks* calls this "unconditional living." Living without conditions means finding our spiritual calm, where no matter what happens, good or bad, we are ok. Without this spiritual calm, we feel happy when things are 'good' and sad or angry when things are 'bad.' This is a common way of living in the western world today creates a feeling of being on a roller coaster.

When we find a place that is beyond thought, however, we can truly roll with life as it flows. Stuckness, trying to control life, staying small out of fear, or just plain old fear, are all the opposites of going with the flow.

You are enough

"When others asked the truth of me, I was convinced it was not the truth they wanted, but an illusion they could bear to live with." —ANAIS NIN

Chew on that one for a second. Where in your life have you created an illusion of yourself so that others could "handle" you, or changed what you said or did depending on who you were with?

In the eye of the horse, this is a passive action, and manipulative in a sense. When I change something I am doing to appease someone or to interest them or get them to like me, I am being passive and incongruent. Incongruent because I am speaking or acting differently than I am feeling. We all know this and we all have done this at some point, even just to avoid conflict. This can set up some major self-trust issues. How do you trust yourself if you are constantly putting your feelings aside in the name of peace, or being liked?

Coming back to horses, one of the things they most dislike is incongruence. Horses feel energy. When they can feel your energy and then they see you acting differently from that, it doesn't make sense to them and they will usually choose to move away from you.

For example, if you're feeling angry about something and come to a horse pretending to be feeling sweet and happy, the horse will probably move away, and essentially won't trust you. If you simply acknowledge to yourself and the horse, "I'm feeling super angry today but it has nothing to do with you," that will shift your energy to congruent and authentic.

Raven teaches me about being authentically me because she has no questions about who she is. She is Wild and unapologetic and she teaches me how to be this way. We play together, often with the goal of her letting our Wildness shine. When I ask her to run, she gives this big grunt and then proceeds to flip her head around and prance around the field. Her movement is beautiful and big and comes from within. Her energy when she runs with her tail up and her big black self moving quickly through the fields or forest is arresting. It makes me feel my own Wildness inside. At first, I was terrified of her bigness and her big energy, but now I love it. I celebrate it and go and run with her.

So it's like this: each of us has a soul or inner being, a larger and wider part of ourselves that is connected to both Source and Us. Your soul wants for you joy, health, peace, ease, abundance, and all things good. Our soul is celebrating us. It wants most for us that we express our uniqueness, our individuality out into the world. It wants expansion. There is no expansion in staying small. How can we truly feel accepted and loved for who we are when we have never shown who we really are to the world?

I want to say to all and everyone who reads this: You are enough. If you allow yourself to open yourself to the world, you will flourish. You will begin to trust yourself, and then watch out world! A person who trusts themselves to have their own back is unstoppable.

The horses work in the realm of the Divine Feminine

A woman came one summer for a session. She had arrived on a boat and was staying near our farm. She heard about my business and knew it was important for her to come. The session was pretty calm, as she met the horses and talked about her own experience in her business, saying that she had been going pretty hard with her work lately. She talked about the need to slow down and do less pushing and striving. Also, she was working with people in difficult emotional states, so her work was very draining, and she was feeling ready for a shift.

We then decided to stop talking and let the horses show us what they wanted to. I had her choose one of the horses to lead over to the centre of the field. There we did a few more exercises with symbolism and listening into her soul self. Then, when she asked what the horses wanted to show her, Raven and Piper came and ate grass directly at her feet — both of them. It couldn't have been more obvious that they were showing her the importance of the balance of the masculine and the feminine energies in her life. When I told her this, she melted and said that this was right on, and exactly the confirmation she needed to go back home and make changes in her life and business.

Many people in the world right now are feeling the push to get in alignment with the feminine. The world has been in a very unbalanced masculine state.

So now the horses are bringing forth this important message to us: we need to return to the feminine. We need to connect deeply with the sacredness of life and nature. We need to live in harmony and care for ourselves, each other, and for the earth. The horses know how to do this and they are here to teach us how.

A balance of the Feminine and the Masculine is what is called for at this time. The flow of the feminine and the structure of the masculine is what is asking to be present, powerful, and balanced in the sacral chakra or second energy centre.

Flow

The element of the second energy centre is water. Water is the healer of emotions, and it teaches us to go with the flow. Learning to go with the flow is such a necessary part of our life here on earth, and the horses definitely know it. Horses have emotions and react to them, often in huge ways. Horses feel a myriad of emotions.

If you watch horses closely, though, they act out their emotions, sometimes very subtly with the flick of a tail or the pin of an ear, but sometimes in a huge run around around the whole property, snorting and farting the whole way. But within seconds of calming down, they go back to grazing. This is the difference between horses and humans.

Horses don't carry it. They don't carry grudges or worries or anxiety for long periods of time. Instead, the emotion usually moves through them quickly and they are happy to go back to grazing. They go with the flow. But this isn't the only type of flow that they are here to teach us about. A horse once showed me a different kind of flow, a powerful energetic flow within our bodies. This horse was Libby.

Libby and I met at an animal communication weekend event. We were doing a session with her in the round pen and then let her into the field to eat. We were having an experience with her where we felt what it was like to be Libby and what did she want to show us? I went deep into an experience with her that was so much more than a conversation. I was experiencing what it was like to be her. And unexpectedly, she insisted on showing me what it feels like to flow like the inside of a horse. She was showing me how energy flows through her body and she let me feel it! It was the most magical thing I have experienced and will stay with me always.

I meet with Libby now in meditation and we get back to the place of flow regularly so that I can practice having the energy flow through my body. I know now that on a regular day, I am not flowing within my body. It takes practice and a lot of attention. This practice also puts me powerfully into my body, taking up space emotionally and physically. It's so healing!

Sexuality and creativity

I'm in the bath, and I sink into a meditation about my body. I have been dealing with intense gut issues for months now, after years of digestive problems. The intensity has increased to gut aches all day, and my mood ranges from giving up on all of it, to feeling the shift and the falling away of many old dark belief systems.

My meditations have been so powerful as healing journeys that I keep going back to this tool.

By the time I begin the journey into my heart space, my mind is lassoed and able to focus. When I first enter my heart space, I see a mountain. I feel and know that the mountain represents my body. I see two small caves near the base of the mountain. I enter the first cave; it represents my stomach area, the third energy centre.

The feeling in this cave is extremely dry and arid, devoid of life. I know instantly in my bones as my consciousness stands in this cave, that this dryness is because I have hidden myself for so long. There is no power in this area of my body. There is no juicy aliveness. I have been absent from this part of my body. I then ask my body what it needs for healing of this area. All of a sudden, the whole cave is flooded with water and new growth of green, lively plants sprout from the walls of the cave. The water represents to me the flow of emotion and creativity and feeling. It represents me showing who I really am to the world without hiding. And then I see the life that this creates.

This reminds me of another day when I was in a circle with a group of women. We were focussing on the intention of one of the women who wanted to bring more piano playing into her life, and I had a vision of the deep importance of her creativity and music to all of humanity. I was shown that the energetic vibration of her spending time creating was essential. Since this vision, I have focussed on letting go of old belief systems that keep me doing the supposed "important" things like cleaning instead of creating.

But back to the cave vision. I can see the vital importance to my health that opening myself up to the flow of who I am is going to bring to my life. Water also represents our emotions, so this is telling me to be more open and honest about my emotions.

The meditation continues, and my focus draws to the second cave. As I enter, I know that this cave represents my second energy centre, the area of my womb and lady parts. This cave feels entirely different. It is full of roses and other flowers. It feels soft and floral and flowing. It feels like self love. I know that this means I have done so many years of work on loving myself and healing this part of my being. I am thrilled to see the contrast of this energy centre with my third energy centre, and how this area is so full of joy and ease.

I see into your soul

My husband used to say this about my daughter (his step-daughter): "She unnerves me because she looks so deep into me." I remember the night she was born. She was my first baby, and after a miscarriage and then a pregnancy with lots of nausea, barfing, pepperoni and orange popsicles, she arrived. That first night, they let her lie in the hospital bed with me. I couldn't believe I could have this tiny being sleep next to me and was in absolute awe of this experience. I could have stared at her all night but I was exhausted after 10 long hours of labour so I closed my eyes, but you know that feeling of being watched? Thinking for sure she would be off in newborn sleepland, I opened my eyes to something that makes me cry still as I write this:

When I opened my eyes, all I saw were eyes. These huge dark eyes of mostly pupils were staring into me and seeing my deepest self. She was drinking me in with her eyes. It was one of the most intensely intimate experiences of my life.

This is what it feels like (without the intimate mother/child connection) when a horse looks into you. They see all of you. It feels intensely intimate. There is nowhere to hide in these kinds of relationships. That's why people are afraid of horses. They feel fear at being really seen. We do everything we can to hide, to not be seen in such a deeply intimate way.

These beings see the unseen in us and if we haven't even been brave enough to look at the unseen in us yet, it feels jarring when someone else sees it.

We in the west haven't been taught to show our emotions. We've been taught to hide all of those yucky, uncomfortable parts of ourselves.

Our emotions are our superpowers

This idea of our emotions being our superpowers hit me one day after I had finished six tarot readings for people and found myself saying, "Our emotions are our superpowers" almost every time. What? Superpowers and emotions in the same sentence? Aren't emotions the little beasties that we're trying to tame, trying to stuff down or cover up as soon as they bubble to the surface?

I'm a crier. I can't help it. Things just hit me straight in the heart, the dam cracks, and that's it. Ask my family. Ask my kids. My five-year-old gets extra special excitement by glancing over at me and making a big show of rolling his eyes when he sees the tears flowing. I let myself go when I'm at home with my family, watching TV and movies. What can I say? I'm a big-hearted softie.

But there are times when it's not quite so acceptable. Some of us have gone through life feeling like we are too much — too much passion, too much anger, too much mushiness, too much crying, hearing things like, "Just tone it down would you?" or "You're using crying as manipulation!" What? If I can't cry when

I discuss what I'm feeling emotional about, I'm going to walk out the door and that is the last time we will talk. Some of us just can't Be without being emotional. I am tired of stuffing all this emotion down in my body and suffering physically because of it. I am tired of faking it! How about you?

What I really want to talk about is the stuffing down of emotion. Stuffing sucks. My whole life I have felt like a stuffed turkey, with all this emotion inside, sitting inside an oven that's heating up, burning me from the inside out.

I know I'm not the only one. There are people all over this western free world who are stuffing. I see it in their eyes every day. I can feel the energy bursting from inside them and I can see the emptiness in their eyes.

This is the great joke: our emotions — the ones that we are trying so hard to pretend are not there — are direct messages from our soul. They ARE the path to healing.

There. I said it and now you know. There is no more avoiding it. If you want to heal, emotionally, physically, and/or spiritually, you've got to look at your emotions and begin to befriend them.

Burning through emotion

I sit down to pick a card, and am drawn to the deck that sits below my table: Linda Kohanov and Kim McElroy's "Way of the Horse" cards. I pick card number 33, Bonfire. I've chosen this card not once, but multiple times since I have had the deck. The Bonfire card is about clearing and releasing, and using emotion as fuel for transformation. It says, "A rearing fire horse demands attention, drawing power from his blazing herd."

I was just discussing this with a client the other day: the horses stand in front of us, demanding our attention to the things we are avoiding or not seeing. I have experienced this so many times with Raven, where she calmly but intensely waits, demanding that I see something for what it is. Something that I might be trying to avoid.

The Bonfire card goes on to say, "It's no small task to stay present during intense outbursts of power — whether human, equine, or divinely inspired." The card talks about our resistance becoming a powerful source of fuel for our fire. It discusses the great importance of staying totally present during emotional explosions that we experience and "breathing into the sensation, sending it oxygen and awareness."

This is something that I have struggled with. My ego wants to avoid anything that isn't pretty and nice and acceptable to the world. In early life, our emotions aren't usually embraced by a parent saying, "Yes, let it all flow out, feel your feeling to the bottom! Scream it out, lash it out!"

No, most parents would prefer that emotion come out in gentle quiet sessions, or maybe that it just doesn't come out at all. We, and I do include myself in this, are usually so tired, overworked, or worried that we would prefer our children work out their emotions quietly. But not really!

We really want our kids to belt it out, dance it out, scream it out, pound the pillows! This card discusses how important it is for us to feel and be fully present with our feelings all the way from beginning to end, and as Buddhist master Chogyam Rinpoche says about feelings, "Feel them completely and fully and don't hold back. You live them right through until they have completed themselves." This is the work that the horses are ready to do with us daily in our interactions: the work of alchemy and "turning the lead of earthly experience into soul's gold."

Painting

I want to paint, always have. Painting is so romantic to me. It seems like romance on a page, the colours moving in and out and around each other like a dance, touching and retreating. Blue loves red, snuggles up to it, and then melds with it and they become one, making a new essence, something that wasn't in existence before the two got together.

A brush comes to move things around in their world, but they continually find each other, reaching for the other and pulling it in, swallowing it until it can be seen on the inside of the other.

In romance, partnership, love, we swallow the other, we neutralize, alchemize what we like and try to change what we don't, fighting against it, being critical of it, making ourselves better than those traits, always making ourselves better or worse than something we measure ourselves against.

A painting doesn't reject parts of itself; it accepts every colour, every mark, as a necessary part of the whole. Necessary, accepting, loving, incorporating, assimilating.

Paint is just paint. We are the painting and the paint. We are colours and canvas, we are landscape and paintbrush. Put it all on one canvas. Be. Accept.

Dancing with horses

I talked earlier about how much dance allowed me to open up my sacral chakra, my Feminine, and my Wild. There is a place you can find, when you're following in partner dance, where you can feel your connection to your own soul. That place where you are energetically open and fiercely present in the moment, so that when someone asks you to move left, you easily move left, they ask you to turn and you turn — not because they are controlling you, but because you are so light in your body and so connected to your own soul and to the soul of your partner, that together you are making a third entity, a third dance.

I dance with the horses. I made a video with Raven where I did the salsa dance steps with her. It was amazing! Horses dance with energy, the same way that we can when we are able to get into that soul place within ourselves.

This is the space of oneness. When we find this place and hold it, magic flows in. This is the place where we meet our Wild selves. This is where our soul stands before us and we feel the intensity of the trust of who we really are.

To flow is to be vulnerable

Afraid to love fully and be seen fully
So vulnerable.
Scared to feel vulnerable and be truly seen.
Always trying to hide something.

How do I choose peace?
Let go of fear.
Throw it in the ocean.
Get it out. Let closeness happen.
Let others see the true you.
Throw your barriers away. Be Raw.
Get out of your own way.
Experience the sweetness, the trust, the love.

Flow. Let the water flow through you.
Let yourself open to the flow of water, the flow of touch,
the flow of being.

—THIRZA VOYSEY

Suggestions from the horses for balancing and cleansing the 2nd energy centre:

1. Dance. Move your hips, move your arms, flow, feel, play with the music and let yourself be moved.
2. Create. Humans are made to create. Find all the ways that light your spark and do them. Make bad art! Making bad art is a healing pastime that helps us get out of the state of perfectionism that takes the fun out of creating.
3. Feel your emotions, move, and then go back to grazing.
4. Do the things that bring you delight.
5. Experience more awe in your life.
6. Be near water.
7. Feel into yourself for the flow. What does flow feel like in your body?
8. Feel the inside of your body. Feel the inside of your hips, your belly, your lower back.
9. Feel your spark. Feel how creating brings energy into you and lights you up.
10. Masturbate. Find your g-spot. This is the place of the ancestral feminine. Experience the greater flow of energy that arises from this place.
11. Experience your feelings through all of the senses. For example, what does your anger sound like? What does your grief feel like on your skin or in your belly? What does your joy smell like?

Journaling questions:

- Am I open to change in my life? Can I go with the flow?
- Do I feel guilt or shame?
- Do I have open space and time in my life for creating?
- Do I feel my feelings, allow the message they have to come through, and then let them go?
- Do I honour my sexuality? Do I respect my own boundaries and my needs?
- Affirmation for 2nd energy centre:
  I am Creation here to Create.

3rd Energy Centre/ Solar Plexus

3rd Energy Centre
Solar Plexus

The Wild in the solar plexus chakra or third energy centre feels like sunshine. It's warm and sure and confident and powerful. Your Wild trusts its gut instincts and moves through life connected to this energetic centre. It sees life clearly and makes powerful decisions. It's made up of the element of fire. It has a powerful will to bring its Beingness to the world. The Wild feels the energy of everything through this centre. It feels people and experiences energetically. The Wild here sets strong and sure boundaries around who it is, and refuses to diminish itself for others.

We feel this energy in our stomachs, our digestive systems, and our adrenal glands. The energy is connected to how we "digest" life, and how clearly we are being who we really are. Authenticity and personal power are good words to describe the energy here.

Experiencing Inner Power

I walk into the appointment room, and inside is a shaman from the mountains of Ecuador. My session is starting, and as he speaks to me, I can't look him in the eye. I feel my body start to shake, and I keep looking away. The power of his presence washes over me, and I'm shrinking and falling into myself. I lie on the table fully clothed and the session commences. I remember going into a deep state of meditation while he completes the ceremonial work needed for my next steps.

The session is focussed on my third energy centre, my place of personal power. I have been leaking personal power in an effort to please everyone around me. He is working energetically to help me hold my power within my body. Before the session ends, I see myself standing in a power position with all my ancestors, and his ancestors, and all the ancestors standing behind me. I feel their support, their hands on my back. I feel deeply supported, and I feel my body holding this intense power within it.

As I come back to my body into the room, I find it slow-going. Once I rouse myself and the ceremony is complete, I rise to sitting. As the shaman speaks with me after the session, I am able to meet and hold his intense gaze. I feel my body holding this power within it. For the first time in my life since I was five years old, I feel my wholeness, my power, my soul.

This is what it feels like standing in front of the thousand pound force of a horse. I can feel the intense knowing vibrational presence, and they call for me, and everyone who experiences them, to rise into their own power. Granted, not every animal is so intense, but horses, with their sensitivity to how we feel, are able to see right through our masks. They see our power leaks as clear as day, and they often show them to us — right in our face.

To me, this kind of biofeedback is perfect because horses show us what we can't see in ourselves. When an animal as big as a horse shows you something, you're going to see it. Without these experiences with such an intense presence, we wouldn't have a way to see these aspects of ourselves. It is the fierceness and power of the presence of the horses that really helps us evolve.

Control

"Watch any plant or animal and let it teach you acceptance of what is, surrender to the Now. Let it teach you Being . . . how to live and how to die." —ECKHART TOLLE

Journal entry:

I was out at the barn last night, noticing how much was whirling around in my head about what I "should" teach my horses and what I "need" to do with them every day. It went on and on and on! I stopped to look at my mind. I recognized this feeling of doing, doing, doing; the need to "do" in order to prove myself as a good mother. Aha! I had gotten to the root of it.

I have been so busy trying to prove myself as a "good this," and a "good that," and now for 18 years I've been trying to prove that I'm a good mother. That's it! Now if someone would just crown me Wonderful Mother, I could be happy — right? Not right.

Being crowned "Wonderful Mother" would only make me continue to strive to be perfect, to keep on proving myself to the world, and really, all we are looking for when we're turning ourselves inside out for the false standard of perfectionism is to feel worthy. Phew. That's it. We all want to feel worthy!

Imagine if we lived in a world where there wasn't a false construct set up for us by society and the patriarchy to be something perfect that doesn't exist. Imagine! The freedom to be! Well, I've decided to live in that place.

I know that the more we focus on something, the more it expands, so I am creating a new space to live in, a world where we are unconditionally loved and accepted for who we are, with nothing to do. A world where we are worthy just for being alive and breathing. Living in a world where we are no longer struggling daily to convince everyone of our worthiness is such a free place. It's a place where we can expand and breathe and be fully who we are. It's a place where we can create and express ourselves freely! We can even share who we are with the whole world while having joy in our hearts. In this world, there is only authenticity and creation.

It's also a world where we feel *everything*.

Boundaries

Journal entry:

Before I went to the horses today, I asked the universe to help me with three things: I was asking for clarity about this book experience, information about some physical pain I have been having, and clarity about obsessive thoughts. I went and sat by a cedar tree. I felt deeply grounded and centred. I could feel the flow of the tree moving through me and then this message came, "You are not a tree. You are not a horse. You are human. Be fully human."

Be fully human? What does that even mean? Am I not fully human?

If you are like me, you are missing some filters. Those of us who are really sensitive are so energetically open that we can absorb everything. As children, we probably absorbed the emotions of those around us and didn't know if the emotion belonged to us or to someone else. This is being empathic, but it's not safe. This is what the horses and the cedar tree showed me today. They told me that if I can fully commit to being human, I will be free of pain. They told me the only reason I am having pain is because I spend so much time out of my body.

Since being a child, I have just wanted to meld with nature. Nature feels like a safe place, and I haven't felt safe in my human body, so I wanted to be nature. I wanted to be the trees and the animals that I surrounded myself with.

Today I learned from nature that I am not a tree and I don't want fungus growing on my body, and I'm not a horse and I don't want horse issues. This realization hit me hard. I need to set boundaries between me and the outside world. I have to learn what I never learned, that I am a human and that I have to fully accept that in order to live a full, healthy human life.

And so, sitting with my body pressed against that cedar tree, I surrendered to becoming fully human, and as I took a deep breath into my whole being, I could feel my entire self relax.

Responsibility and high expectations

Horses, like humans living in society, have been taught to be responsible. We have been taught that we must meet the expectations of others, initially, and then later, ourselves. These are often very high expectations — and often hard to meet — which becomes a self sabotage situation. We set expectations for ourselves, don't meet them, and then beat ourselves up. It can become a dangerous downward spiral.

We do the same with horses. We set expectations of what they'll do with us, and when they don't perform as we expect, we get frustrated or angry with them and try to gain more control. This leaves horses confused, nervous, and untrusting of us — and sometimes themselves.

Raven has a nervous habit of putting her head down and suckling like she would as a foal, when she is asked to do something. She does this less and less as time goes on here at the farm. She is learning new lessons from us. She is learning that we will not hurt her if she doesn't do as we ask. As we become more experienced with her, she is learning that we won't even get frustrated with her if she says no. She is learning that responding to requests from humans can even lead to fun things — like carrots!

What Raven is most interested in though (well, honestly, it is the carrots), is the energy with which we present her with requests. If she is being asked with no expectations if she would like to engage, she can feel the lack of expectation behind something and is more interested in responding. This is a slow process and takes much patience on my part, but it is so important.

We don't know the details of Raven's life before she came to us. She was 11 when she arrived, so she had had many experiences with humans before she knew us. As a previous racehorse and probably a broodmare (mama), we have no idea how she was treated. We can, however, get a good idea of where she was not respected or given choice by her behaviour when we work with her.

I had a conversation with my youngest son that described this experience of horses just wanting to show us who they are without us having all our human expectations of them. I asked, "What do horses teach us?" And he answered, "They teach us to be who we are."

Suggestions from the horses for balancing and cleansing the 3rd energy centre:

1. Let the sun shine on you. Five minutes of letting the sun shine on your closed eyes is so healing and stimulating for your pineal gland (see 7th energy centre).
2. Pay close attention to when you are not Shining Who You Are, but instead are masking yourself for someone in your life or for society. Burn the masks.
3. Notice when you are taking on the emotions of others. Often empaths will take on the emotions of others, and you need a filter for this. Boundaries help to keep the

emotions of others out of your energetic system.

4. Learn emotional and physical boundaries. This is one of the biggest lessons that the horses teach. Don't take on what isn't yours, and be quick, sure, and clear about your boundaries.
5. Let go of responsibility from the past and learn instead to respond in the present.
6. Learn and practice trust and confidence with horses.
7. Let go of "shoulds."
8. Are there things you want to do, but are afraid? Make powerful decisions and then watch the old stories that come up.
9. Let go of control. Trust that everything is always working out.
10. Understand that life brings you lessons for you to learn about yourself. Embrace the lessons and thank them.
11. Allow life to move you and bring you to your knees. See the magic and beauty in every single experience.

Journaling questions:

- Do I express my anger assertively, or aggressively or passive-aggressively?
- Do I try to control life out of fear of losing control?
- Do I put my needs last? Do I want people to see me as being able to handle everything?
- Am I willing to be more vulnerable?
- Am I confident that I can handle adversity in my life? Why or why not?
- Affirmation for 3rd energy centre: I am authentic power.

4th Energy Centre/ Heart Chakra

4th Energy Centre
Heart Chakra

The Wild is written on the walls of your heart. —THIRZA VOYSEY

The heart is the natural home of the Wild. The Wild in the heart chakra is the direct, powerful connection between spirit and earth. We are the place where spirit and earth meet, and the heart is where the connection happens. Connection is a word that lives in this centre.

In our Wild state, we are all so deeply connected to each other. Connection is another word for love. The Wild in the heart is the energy of love, compassion, and understanding.

This is also the centre of self-love. The horses know everything about self-love. They have no other way. They love themselves and each other deeply and intensely, but they don't show it in the ways we expect. The Heart Math Institute says that "the heart has electrical signals up to 60 times stronger, and a magnetic field 5000 times more powerful than the brain." Most of us live our lives mostly in our heads and in the place of fear. The horses encourage us to live in our hearts and to live from love. When we work with the horses, we start to hear the whispers of the soul as we spend more time in connection with our heart.

Joy melts the walls around the heart

I have decided to become addicted to joy. Joy is a high-vibe emotion and it creates health and abundance. Besides, it's so much more fun to be joyful than negative!

I kept getting this card in the Tarot that depicts an addiction to negativity, and I thought, "No way! I'm so positive! I'm so positive that negativity drives me nuts! When people are negative or see the glass half empty, I get so annoyed!" Exactly. Why does it drive me nuts? Because what you judge most about another is within yourself. Wammo. That was a hard one to swallow.

Me, negative? Then it hit me: I realized that worrying is negativity and that's something I've done for most of my life. Worrying has been my go-to. It's been my way to feel in control of my life.

But finding joy calls for a letting go of how we usually think about things, a faith in the importance of feeling good, and a commitment to self-love.

As kids, we all believe in fun and laughter and joy. Where does that go? Someone once told me when I was in university, "Find something you love to do and find someone to pay you to do it." I ignored that for a while and did what was expected of me.

I got a great job with the government as a social worker and did that for 11 years, hating it most days. I couldn't make sense of all the barriers that were being put up when our jobs were to help people. I wanted to help people in a way that I felt like I was really helping them and not throwing policy and red tape at them.

So I finally got the courage to leave — and that was when I committed to myself that I would only do what I love. I took yoga teacher training and embarked on a life of making it on my own, but that is really hard to do when you still have those old beliefs about how society works. You see, I knew deep inside that I could do what I love and that people who needed my services would find me, but I didn't have the courage or self-esteem to stay committed when things became overwhelming or scary.

Since embarking on my own businesses, with every creative act I put out there, whether it's a course I'm offering or a blog post I'm writing, I've felt like I'm taking my intestines from inside me and hanging them out in the world for people to look at and judge and criticize. This, obviously, is not a comfortable feeling. I had the belief in doing what we love, but I was missing the belief that I could be abundant and support my family while doing it. It's been years since leaving the safety of a government job and I'm still reconciling my beliefs about the feasibility of following my bliss.

But as *Abraham-Hicks* says, *"You cannot struggle to joy. Struggle and joy are not on the same channel. You joy your way to joy. You laugh your way to success. It is through your joy that good things come."* So I have decided to joy my way to joy!

When I write or create or put myself out there in my business, I notice a huge cloud of perfectionism and fear of failure hanging over me. So I have decided that if I focus on the fun of writing, of creating, of showing people who I am and what I do, I shall succeed. And what is success, but joy?

The horses remind me daily to keep following my joy. They do look at me sideways when I dance and sing around them, but I know they love the energy of it. I see them soften with the energy of joy, and in those moments, I know that we are not protecting our hearts with walls, but softening and opening our hearts with love.

The Haunted Heart

The heart sits at the core of me,
Minding its own business
I run from it across the years of my life
Until I stumble and trip off the cliff,
Tumbling, grasping, groping in the dark
Looking for something to hold onto
To ground myself with, a rock, an edge, a tree.
But there is nothing.
The heart is deep and full of caverns with no light.
I hit the bottom and melt into the darkness.
I am lying on the damp cold earth at the bottom of the cavern
I curl up, protecting myself from the dark and the cold.
But then, I breathe.
I inhale the scent of the earth deeply into the depths of my nose
I lay my body open and surrender to the earth below
I feel everything.
A soft gentle rhythmic pounding inside of me
The walls around my senses melt away
And there is just my being and my heart
We feel each other.
We know each other
I am home.

—THIRZA VOYSEY

The haunted heart

I worked in a reportedly haunted house for a short time as a social worker. I was in an office by myself on the top floor. Because I believed the house to be haunted, I kept all my senses and energy pulled into myself. I kept my eyes down, I breathed shallowly. I shut down all of my normal fully awake senses. I didn't want to sense anything! I threw a wall up in front of my feeling centre so that nothing came in and nothing went out. I didn't want to sense anything scary because I didn't think I could handle it, and I didn't want to attract anything out of the shadows by being my big, loud self.

This is how we act in fearful situations. We don't want to know, see, hear, smell, taste, or touch anything scary. We all know this feeling of holding ourselves tightly, like a little mouse trembling in the corner of a dark room so no one will see us, waiting for the moment of escape.

This is exactly how I behave with my very own haunted heart. As soon as I walk through the doors and into that vast chamber, I feel terror run through me. Unless I quickly find light and joy and positivity in there, I am immediately huddled in a corner, shutting down my senses in an attempt not to feel anything. I don't want to feel anything. There are some big, scary ghosts hanging out in there. My fear is that once I see them and notice them and acknowledge that they are there, I will have to face them — and what if I can't? What if I'm not strong enough to endure what I find? So when the heart starts talking to me, I shrink from it. I ignore it. I pretend it wasn't talking to me. I avoid eye contact. I recede into myself.

Why are you protecting your heart?

I went for a tune-up with my acupuncturist. She told me my weakest organ on that day was my heart. She talked about my posture and my position of defensiveness. "Why," I ask myself, "is my body defending itself? What am I defending myself from? Why am I hunching and protecting my heart? Where am I not feeling safe?"

I came to this earth with a big open heart. But then I thought that the world wasn't really ready for what was in my heart. People aren't always comfortable with the flow of love and joy that comes from a child. There is a lot of "too muchness," and children often get shut down and asked to be quiet and calm down.

When we shut down our hearts, we shut down our outpouring of what's in there. We close down the creative magic that really is each one of us. But when we close down, we're starving the world of everything that is US!

Everything for me right now is about surrendering my mind and living from my heart. Life comes to me when I'm ready. And I'm ready. I want to allow my heart to open and spill out all that I am onto the page and onto the canvas and into the world.

So the universe has begun to whisper to me about painting, and poetry, and flow, and slow moments of allowing and writing. To allow creation to move through me and out of my heart, I need to quiet my mind.

I had a dream that I was a remote-control bug. I was jumping up from the ground to fly, flying high into the sky, and enjoying the thrill of it. But then I felt a force just as strong as my excitement to fly. I could feel myself struggling against something big. I realized in my dream that someone or something was controlling me remotely. They were trying to control me, and I could viscerally feel the struggle against being controlled. I was trying to fly, but was being held back. This dream was the best way for me to feel the external control that I sometimes allow to take hold and diminish all that I am. No more!

I open. I surrender. The horses show me how. I go outside and ask them to show me their open hearts. They look at me sideways and nuzzle into each other, then Raven blows into my nostrils. With that blow, I feel the intensity of her big heart and her acceptance of me as I am.

Something we often don't understand about horses is their fierce love for us. We think that because they act aloof and are often not wanting to be snuggled or hugged, that they don't love us. The opposite is true. When they are in our lives and we theirs, they hold a fierce present love for us.

Raven tells me she holds the strongest space for me to rise into who I really am. She, like me, sees the soul selves of people and others. She sees this so powerfully and holds space for us to rise to meet it. I imagine she often wonders what the heck we are doing stumbling around in the dark when we could just be radiating who we really are.

Perfectionism closes our hearts

I used to be so judgemental. It turns out you can't be intensely perfectionistic with yourself and not be judgemental of others! As mentioned, I was very rigid in how I saw things for myself and others. In structuring these rigid guidelines of how life should be, I had built walls around my heart.

I saw this in interactions with my husband. I was watching myself during my cycle. I was seeing how distinctly different I was during my open, sexual, loving, feminine, first days of my cycle and how, after I ovulated, I was quickly moving back into this unbalanced masculine, walled, rigid, structured, judgemental, world. I became fascinated watching myself go through these two vastly different ways of being month after month.

I started to pay close attention to my thinking during these times, and realized that not only was I miserable during the latter parts of my cycle, but I was separating myself from others. I had thought I was diving into my intuition during these times and that I just wanted to be in a cave with my intuition and my creativity, but in truth, I was allowing a veil of structure and rigidity to lay itself across my body, mood, and life.

And so, like I do when things don't sit right with me, I went to the horses. They showed me my heart.

Rainbow is the colour of the heart

Today, I feel myself bursting open. Like, if I let myself go, I might just explode my rainbow colours all over everything and everyone. I've kept myself small and tight for so long. A little crack of permission to expand feels so inviting and so terrifyingly vulnerable at the same time.

The permission came yesterday on a walk with Izzy, our dog. We were on a hike with no boundaries, our favourite kind of outing. We had nowhere to be. We could just allow the adventure to unfold. As I do on these adventures, I asked the universe and my soul for some clarity, this time around my creative process, my art and writing. And then I walked and trusted that the answers would come.

I dropped into a state of meditation and opened my heart to connect with the moment and the nature around me. In my meditation, I met with my future self. She was wild and confident, an artist and writer. She said, "I am a writer." "What do you write?" I asked her. "Whatever comes through me," she said.

I had always thought of books as a teaching method. I'd thought of my work as teaching, and my role as "teacher," but as the vision switched to "artist," there was no longer anything for me to do. This was so freeing! This idea of channelling my own soul was a new one for me. I had tried so hard to fit my writing into the structure of a book, to make sense, be inspirational, and be understood. But, allowing Source and the voices of the horses to flow through me onto the page? That felt like ease.

Being authentically me and showing that to the world feels like freedom and like I am the prism, showing all of my rainbow colours to the world!

Wellbeing is our natural state

"Be so fully filled up by the intense presence of the moment that you open and surrender, letting it fill you, expand you, ravish you." —ECKHART TOLLE

Our source knows that we are joyful by nature. Wellbeing and bliss are our natural states. Yet so often we keep ourselves far from this.

One morning, on my way home from dropping my son at school, I heard a guy talking on the radio in his "pump you up for Monday" voice. He said, "I'm gonna get you through the week," and he gave a kind of overwhelmed grunt in support of all those people in the hated place of "Monday morning."

I thought, "What is this? What is this disgruntled attitude about life that we have adopted as normal? We seem to have this collective idea that life needs to be hard and that when we work our butts off and do more things that we dislike, it makes us worthy. I know this is in many of us, because I see it in people and I see it in myself. This is probably one of the greatest things that I push against.

I have always believed in my heart that we can do what we love and be abundant in the doing of it. I could always feel that our natural state is joy and this is what we deserve, but I was confused about why we weren't living that truth. I have looked around and seen so many unhappy people, especially unhappy with their work and wondered, "What is going on? Is this really how it's supposed to be?"

So now here I am, creating my dream, spending my days as I choose, and celebrating myself for creating this amazing life. But I still find myself waking up with a cloud hanging over me, with the feeling of not being good enough, and that something isn't right.

So, with no more distractions (after moving to the farm on this little island in the Pacific there are not many distractions left to keep one from looking deep into oneself and one's motives), I asked myself, "What is this cloud? Is it depression? Anxiety? Why, when I have the daily life that I dreamed of, with horses and goats in my front yard, doing meaningful work that I love, with a family and loving relationships, why am I still waking up under this cloud?"

I then realized that the cloud was just my thoughts about what I am doing, my leftover belief systems about this and that, and whether things are good or bad. Judgment, worry, unsettledness, ungroundedness — these were the emotions and feelings that were sitting there when I really looked at why I was waking up sad.

So, with the realization that I needed to let go of old belief systems that were keeping me stuck in old patterns of feeling "not good enough," I decided to go on a joy hunting expedition daily. Of course, my mind told me this was something I didn't have time for, and that I had all of these things to do that were more important than my own joy, but I quickly realized that this was not true.

I actually found myself having a conversation with my husband about how we don't value emotional work and spiritual work nearly as much as we value the "actual" work that we get paid for. I harped on him about this and drove home my belief that emotional, intuitive, mental, and spiritual work are the most important work that we're doing here on earth, and the rest is just filler. I got mad and judgemental about his lack of belief in this, and his belief that we have to turn ourselves inside-out, working our butts off to get anywhere.

And then, in the middle of our heated conversation, I realized that I, too, had these exact same beliefs, but that it was so much easier to externalize my whole belief system onto him and make him the bad guy. So much easier!

When I accepted all of this within myself and made joy my daily priority, everything changed. Now I go for walks and call them my "Joy Hunting" walks. I tell the universe that I am going to go walking in nature and I will not stop or return to the house until I have been hit in the chest by my joy.

Sometimes it feels just like that. I'll spend the first few minutes or longer of my walk, fuming and festering about this situation and that, with worry, worry, stress, stress . . . and then, I'll feel like just standing by a tree or staring up into the sky — and I feel it. It hits me right in the chest: JOY! Sometimes it feels big and expansive, sometimes it feels like awe, and sometimes it feels like quiet appreciation of the beauty of nature. All of these things are my joy.

So I ride the wave. I ride the wave of appreciation throughout my walk, and it just feels so good. Then I go back home, or to town, or dive into whatever activity is mine for the day, and it works better than if I hadn't started my day by going "joy hunting."

These are some of my biggest secrets to mental health:

- Accept that joy is my natural state and that I deserve wellbeing, health, wealth and joy (this step can be one that needs a lot of focus).
- Find joy daily.
- If joy-hunting seems hard or too big, start with appreciation. Write lists of things to appreciate.
- Cultivate self-awareness. Mindful awareness. What is my mind doing? How about now? And now? Where are my thoughts now?
- Make joy a priority.

There is one more thing. As humans, when we think about the things that bring us joy, we are usually looking at the world around us. We are asking, "Is my life good? Do I have the things I want? Is this or that right with my life?" But that is conditional joy, and we are talking here about unconditional joy.

Unconditional joy is when we feel joy just because We Are. I feel joy just because I'm alive. I feel joy because I look out of these human eyes and see so many things that are amazing. I feel joy because I feel awe. I feel joy because I can feel. I feel joy because of the awe-inspiring experience of being alive.

Watch children. They know this. They know joy for its own sake. They know about giggling for no reason, and loving magic because magic rocks. They know that farts are funny and seriousness isn't. They know. Watch them. Watch animals. They know about calmness, peacefulness, and ease. This is joy. Dogs know the wiggly, happy-to-see-you-after-you-were-gone-for-five-minutes-joy. All animals seem to know lie-in-the-sun-and-soak-it-up joy.

Joy doesn't always have to be loud and rambunctious. It can be quiet contentedness. No matter what form it takes, joy is our natural way. Joy is our natural state.

Surrender

"Find love with someone who loves you for your free spirit, someone who has no intention of restricting your wild side but someone who wants to set it free and run with you."

—WILD WOMAN SISTERHOOD

I had two common stories growing up: "I am too much," and "Nobody understands me." I carry these through life, believing them to be true and super-imposing them over all of my relationships. Because of these fears of being too much and not being accepted for who I am, I hid who I really was for a long, long time.

One of my biggest fears was not to be accepted by my people and to be abandoned as a result. So I adapted and hid and morphed the real me. I curled myself up in a ball, trying to fit into other peoples' boxes so much and for so long that I almost stayed like that. Like a poster that has been curled up for a long time, I almost didn't uncurl. Between stuffing myself into the life created for me and holding myself tightly rigid, it was almost too much for me.

But then I met horses and realized that in holding myself tight and rigid, and keeping my true self inside, I was acting like a predator to them. The horses showed me that they can't trust me when I'm hiding myself. They took me on a journey of opening and showing who I really am. They showed me how to be comfortable within my own energetic bubble. When your body is filled with anxiety, you hold it tight.

When you're afraid of the world and what might happen if you show who you really are, you hold your true self close to your chest. When you don't trust others to accept you, you lie to them about who you are. Hiding ourselves is essentially lying, and there's nothing to be trusted in someone who has learned to be constantly lying. I would never have admitted that I was being dishonest if someone other than a horse had told me that. But when I can feel something that huge sitting as a wedge between me and a horse, I am committed to working on it.

It has happened a few times that horses don't fully trust me because I'm not trusting myself fully to be open to the world. It wasn't until I was working with Luna in training, though, that the issue was staring me right in the face. There are so many horse trainers out there and so many methods. I'm not one who cares about methods, though, as you may have noticed.

My measuring stick for whether I will accept or reject something in my life is this: "Does this feel in alignment with me and my way of being? Does my whole being get a 'yes' when I do this thing?" And when it comes to the "horse training" methods that I have been exposed to so far, I'll take bits from each method, but nothing has totally felt right to me yet.

When something doesn't sit right with me, I'm left with a question. And that's exciting, because behind a question is a door. And behind the door is a whole journey.

In this case, the question is: When I ask Luna to do something, like run around me in a circle, and she refuses, is the answer to ask her louder and with more pressure? Or is there another answer?

I know there's another answer, and so I leap off onto a new journey of curiosity to find it. This is how my life has gone. I use my intuition to notice if something doesn't feel right to me. And in my search so far I've learned this: It's my job to show myself to the horse. I must stand in the space and be in the centre of my energetics circle. When I am powerfully in my own body and energy, I can clearly ask the horse something.

As trainer *Josh Nichols* says, it's not about becoming louder or using bigger cues, it's about being more honest. Luna is teaching me and calling from me to be more honest with myself and with her.

Honesty itself is a big journey. When we trust the world around us, we can trust it and our heart can flow open. If we think about the 5th energy centre and the 3rd energy centre, the throat and the solar plexus, we see the connection between integrity (5th) and personal power (3rd). The throat calls for us to bring to the outside what's on the inside. It calls for us to be clear and honest without changing or hiding things. This action relates to our solar plexus or place of power, because if we're not showing who we are honestly, we aren't powerful.

When I handed my personal power to the other members of my family, that part of me lost energy and started to have symptoms like difficult digestion, and body pain. This loss of energy continued as I grew up and kept trying to live my life to please others. It was like a constant energy drain.

I got some of my power back as I started to trust that my Soul had a plan for me and when I started to make choices for my own soul self.

Breathe

"Go where you breathe free." —BUTTERFLIES RISING

I was ready to give up. It was one of those days where I felt deep overwhelm, waking up feeling crappy in a chaotic world with a mind full of fear. I was out feeding the horses and heard the word "Breathe". I looked over and saw Raven looking right at me with her ears perked up. I felt the intense impact of this message like it was the answer to everything. I know I don't breathe properly. I am a chest breather. Even after years of yoga and pranayama, I still feel the tightening when I try to breathe deeply.

When I drop in and focus on allowing the air to flow into all the nooks and crannies of my body, I can breathe, but in my regular day to day living, I realized that Raven was right. I wasn't breathing.

For breath to really flow, we have to be intensely, fiercely present within our bodies. Horses know this. Horses live in the centre of every moment. They hold their breath when they're stressed and breathe freely when they're calm. When they've accepted something and relaxed about it, they blow all their breath out in a big, loud sigh.

For me to breathe free, my mind has to be free. This hasn't been the case until recently. It works both ways: practicing breathing frees my mind, and doing practices to free my mind frees my breathing.

I sit in my rocking chair at the barn, listen to the horses munch their yummy hay and practice, allowing the breath to flow deeply into my being.

What I've learned about this is that to truly be at ease, our energy body has to be balanced. This is what Raven meant when she told me to breathe.

To breathe is to allow life force into all the deep parts of ourselves. This, for some, is terrifying. Allowing life force to touch all the tender vulnerable parts of ourselves feels intimate. We are allowing life to deeply touch us.

For anyone who has been traumatized (all of us in some way, just by living in our society), this feels absolutely terrifying. When we have experienced trauma, we build huge walls around our hearts and our souls — our most vulnerable parts.

Suggestions from the horses for balancing and cleansing the 4th energy centre:

1. Find your joy and find it often.
2. Connect with animals through your heart.
3. Find your heart cave and go there in meditation often to see what your Wild wants to tell you.
4. Practice sitting with the horses and feeling inside your heart. Connect your heart to the horse's heart with your imagination.

5. Breathe deeply.
6. Practice relaxing your entire being. Sit comfortably and relax parts of yourself that you never pay attention to: the skin behind your ear, the muscles between your ribs, etc.
7. Keep your heart lifted physically. So many have learned to protect their hearts through hunching physically. Open, open, open.
8. Allow yourself to be loved. Sit with a horse and allow the intense love that flows from all horses flow into your heart. Accept it.
9. Learn to receive. Many human issues come from you not letting love in. The feelings of unworthiness block all the goodness that is trying to flow into your life. Let it in.
10. Open yourself to love. Allow yourself to be loved.
11. Stand naked in front of the world (metaphorically or physically if you want).

Journaling questions:

- Do I believe that I deserve to unconditionally love myself and to forgive myself?
- Do I feel comfortable speaking words of love to others and to myself?
- Can I practice saying loving words to myself and having loving thoughts about myself more often?
- Do I believe that I have to do things to earn love or do I know that I am worthy of love just because I exist?
- Do I have a heavy heart? Can I journal about grief or disappointments that I have about my life?
- Affirmation for 4th energy centre: I am Love.

5th Energy Centre/ Throat Chakra

5th Energy Centre
Throat Chakra

The 5th energetic centre, located in the throat, holds the energy of integrity, the truth of your soul, speaking your truth, and listening deeply to the sounds of Spirit. The Wild here feels like connection through communication, like listening intently for the Wild within us. It involves intuitive listening, sitting quietly, being in the body, and knowing what is out of integrity in ourselves, the world, and in others. The energy is subtle yet powerful.

The energy of the world right now is calling for us to live from our hearts and speak our truths. It is imperative that we walk our talk in the world. We will be shown loudly in our lives where we aren't living from love. This also means we need to be showing our insides on the outside, through clear speech and creativity.

I find that the horses are brilliant at showing us these places where we are out of integrity. I make sure I am always deeply listening so I don't miss their wisdom with this. This is so important. We are all being called to come out of hiding and show our true Wild to the world at this time. This is the work. If we follow the path of this energy centre, we will find all the reasons for any states of dis-ease within us. We can listen so deeply to our bodies from this centre, that we can find any imbalance within us.

Shamanic journeying through the wheel

I was once involved in a class where we were doing a shamanic journey for healing. Drumming was used as the carrier, and as soon as the drumming started, I saw myself on the back of a black horse, and the drum was the sound of the horse's hooves. The mare ran with me on her back, and we jumped together into a lake. As we rose out of the lake, we were in another world. I looked behind me and I could see the world we had come from as an upside down world at the bottom of the lake.

Once out of the lake, the black horse started to run again with me on her back. Then I switched, and I was an eagle, flying above the earth. I flew up and up until I was connected to All That Is, the planets, and the other galaxies. Then I felt myself falling and tumbling, unafraid. As I gently reached the ground, I shape-shifted again into a small mouse, crawling along on the earth, seeing the world up close. Suddenly, I shifted again and felt myself stealthily moving through the forest as a black panther.

The path I was following opened to a clearing; there were 12 women gathered around the fire at the centre. The women were telling me, as the panther, that I had to join them and speak my truth. My story and my truth were needed to complete the circle.

When the drumming started to slow, I became myself again and was on the back of the black horse. We ran, more slowly this time, and jumped in the lake. As we re-emerged, I felt the image of the black horse fade and I was back in my body, in the room. As the drumming stopped, we recalled our visions and were encouraged to write them down.

The instructors explained that in shamanic journeys, as in dreams, the most important part is how you feel during the journey; how the events make you feel. I realized that on the black horse, I had felt supported and guided. When I was an eagle, I felt free and wise and connected to the universe. When I was a mouse, I felt an incredible sense of presence while I was experiencing the world close up, and I felt a deep connection with the earth. When I was a panther, I felt peace, strength, and power. When the 12 women told me that my wisdom and voice were needed to complete the circle, I felt self-worth and focus. I felt the will to write and speak the truth coursing through me like a passionate surge.

Honesty

"Never apologize for showing feeling. When you do so, you apologize for the truth." —BENJAMIN DISRAELI

Journal entry:

Honesty comes from deep within. It's a connection so deep and sure. Sometimes the first time we know our truth is when we hear ourselves speaking it out loud.

Truth comes from above and below, from other places, other lives. It grabs hold of us and screams itself out. If it doesn't get out, it just chews itself through us from the inside.

Honesty burns from the inside out. Lack of honesty makes holes. Honesty frees itself through the 5th energy centre at the throat. We hear our truth then we speak it or yell it. It only comes when we open up and step out of the way. We can plug our own 5th energy centre our whole lives and in so doing, we can keep it shut, plugged, clogged with black sludge and fear like a bathroom sink. Fear is a heavy, thick energy.

My body at 30 was filled with fear. I felt heavy, filled with heavy energy and thoughts. My mind felt clogged and foggy.

I couldn't see past my fear in any way. Every experience, every relationship, was surrounded with fear. I marinated in it. My body ached. It didn't want to move. My bones stuck to each other and to themselves. The pain shot through my back and sent me to the floor in tears, unable to move. I was in a spasm of fear. This was a moment of reckoning. Carry on in fear — or change.

The universe tried yelling at me, but I didn't listen. I continued on my ego way, ignoring my body, running because it would keep me skinny and "perfect." It didn't matter to me what truths I wasn't facing, or what harm I was causing my body. Perfection was the ultimate goal.

The image or illusion of perfection, is a very, heavy picture to hold up for one's entire life. At 30, my lower back was sore, it was cracking under the strain. And with it, my "perfect" image of myself was starting to blur. Whenever I felt this image start to falter, I would obsess more intensely, thinking, "What does my tummy look like? How much does it stick out below my belly button? How much fat did I eat today? I'm really hungry so I'll snack on no-fat chips and eat the whole bag."

Obsessed with food and exercise, I would run and run and run, past my aching back and failing body, past all the signs to stop. Running made me feel strong.

Really what was happening was that my ego was very strong. I could run farther and faster than most people I knew, and that made me feel strong. I could beat them in a race, so I must be a strong person. The illusion ran deep and for a long time.

While I was at university, no one was watching. I could obsess long and hard about my eating and exercise. No one told me how much to eat or when to stop running. I was not going to gain the "Freshman 15," I was actually going to lose it. I wasn't going to suffer like everybody else.

Little did I know, I was suffering the most. I was screaming to be set free from this madness of restriction and structure. There was a little ME inside that I wasn't even hearing, let alone acknowledging. I wasn't even at the point of ignoring her yet. I didn't even know she existed.

Hiding

One day, a woman came for a Horse Medicine session. The energy around her was one of hiding. The horses got right to helping her by doing some energetic work around her family of origin where her hiding had begun. This work was powerful for her and she started the work of feeling worthy enough to show who she really is to the world and to share her gifts.

I know this energy of hiding well. The world knows this energy well. If we aren't connected, we're hiding, and it's an unnatural energy. It's not our Wild selves showing up.

The horses don't hide who they are. They are who they are and they are unapologetic about it!

This got me thinking about the ways that I hide (a topic I've looked at many times, but here I was again, face to face with it).

I hid because it wasn't safe to be who I was in the world. Belonging is a deep, instinctual need of all animals, including us humans. When we show up on the planet in our early years and we aren't accepted and celebrated for who we are, we start to shut down and we are who we think the world wants us to be. We become grey versions of who we are.

I didn't know this was an issue for me. I'm really good in social situations — or I think I am — so I thought I was being real with the world, but really, I was not. I have been hiding so much of me, and the closing down starts as soon as emotion shows up for me.

When I speak about emotion, I feel uncomfortable and I shut down. I didn't realize how much I did this until I took a singing lesson.

My voice is good and I can hit the notes, but my voice was stuck in fear. I was unbalanced like crazy. When my instructor and I did exercises to open my voice up, I felt naked and vulnerable. She told me to stop shutting my eyes when I sing because it shuts down my voice. I can see now how I do that every time I talk about something emotional, and for sure every time I sing! This realization was intense for me!

I could feel how much of a habit this was when singing, and I realized that when I talk to people, I often look away repeatedly during the conversation for a "break." I also noticed, as I was practicing singing to my horse Raven, that I was glazing my eyes over, and instead of sending the sound to her, I was blocking it. Blocking me.

I see this in many people who grow up in situations or have relationships where people around them are emotionally closed. These people, as a result, often don't have the energetic and emotional strength to hold big emotions in a conversation, and so they disconnect.

The world is in project-disconnect right now. We disconnect from life with our electronics, and our busy lives, our striving, and our accumulation of things.

Life is different when we live in the centre of each moment. Everything changes when we connect with our bodies and our souls in the present. When we do this, when we are embodied and connected, we are full of who we are. We are full of the creation of ourselves and we know that sharing that creation with the world is our most important work.

Integrity

Luna bit me one morning during feeding. I was walking past her with a bucket of water for Piper's mash, and she reached out while eating her hay and bit me. Hard! She bit me right on my breast and raked her teeth across my nipple. It ached every time it touched my shirt. I was furious! I wasn't furious because it was the *first time* she had bitten me out of nowhere. I was furious because it was the *third time* she had bitten me in the same place!

I was so mad and so shocked! It's been a while since the last time, so I had chalked it up to "newcomer jitters." I didn't want to be so mad, but I was so shocked and in so much pain this time that I couldn't help it.

I threw the empty rubber food dish at her and missed. I cried a lot. I stood by her while she continued eating and told her that this was not okay and that she will not do that again. But the whole time, I knew in my bones that she was trying hard (and not very subtly) to tell me something.

This might sound crazy, like I have a dangerous or bratty horse that I simply need to deal with or "get control of." But I knew. I just knew. So I went inside and once I settled down, I asked Source to show me what this was about. I knew I'd get an answer because I always do.

People might not understand this if they haven't been living with thousand-pound animals, but I've got to tell you — in my experience, there is almost always something for us to learn. You will feel it if there isn't.

In this work, I have to be intensely tapped into the horses so that I can feel whether we're going this way or that, or whether something is physical, emotional, or spiritual. I have also asked for a lot of help. My doubt in these areas has been huge, like anyone's would be. I often find myself asking my mentors (it's so important to have mentors in this work!) because I don't always trust myself enough, but not this time. My intuition was telling me that this was for me, Luna, and my own soul to work out.

So I sat down with the cards. I have read tarot cards for many years and I now use one tarot deck and about five different oracle cards to give a rounded out story about whatever is going on. As I dealt the cards, I knew inside me that this was going to be a very very telling reading.

Before I finish this part of the story, though, some more background information: I have had muscle pain on my right shoulder blade for a few years, which is a long time to have pain in one area. I have done lots of healing modalities, but the pain continues, which I understand as a message for me. The pain sometimes takes over the whole right side of my upper torso, and radiates up into my neck and around into my chest.

The first time Luna bit me, it was in the back, right on the shoulder blade where I was sore. The second time was on the right breast, although pretty gently. This time was a much harder bite and such specific aim!

So I knew that Luna was getting impatient with me and the way I was ignoring the message from my body. I could sense the answer, the story that my shoulder was telling me, hovering around out there in the ether, but I hadn't been able to really nail it down.

So back to the reading. The first card was the Dragonfly. The Dragonfly is about illusion, and I have a lot of illusion in my mind (as do most of us), so it can sometimes be difficult to see deep within myself and the true way forward. This is entirely why I rely heavily on my intuition and why I have been so determined to learn how to trust it and run my life by it. Illusion is heavy in our world.

It was one message from Dragonfly that really hit me in the heart: "Are you trying to prove that you have power," . . . but "are you caught in an illusion that weakens your true feelings or minimizes your abilities?" Yes and yes!

But the last card was the one that really got me. My intuition about this issue has been about sharing my heart with the world (masculine side of my body, sharing outside myself). This last card was about Elk and the importance of integrity.

Integrity is about being authentic to the core. It's a high calling of the 5th energy centre. It is about walking your talk. The Elk card or Elhaz, in the "Earth Warriors Oracle" by *Alana Fairchild*, says that the norse Runic teachings of Elhaz brings Elk wisdom. "This is the soul quality of integrity which places you on the "right" side of the spiritual laws of the universe". Integrity is about sharing your insides clearly on the outside, without changing what you show to the world to suit others.

I am sharing this because it's so important for us to feel our way forward in alignment with our soul and our heart. I have talked about hiding, and feeling disempowered, and being afraid to be my big, spiritual self out there in the world. I know many of us have ancestral fears of being "burned at the stake," or "attacked for our powers," and so we don't show them to the world.

Using my intuition in my work to help people find their inner power is my calling, and maybe whatever you are hiding from the world is your calling. This is my permission for you to do the thing. Do the thing that feels right in your heart, and it will call to hearts all around the world. And it will, in fact, heal you!

The lesson that Luna has for me isn't finished yet, though. There is another part of this that relates to Luna specifically and her "training." She is four years old, and so I expect to "train" her.

I see the integrity issue coming up in this situation as well. I have experienced many different methods of training, before my time as a "horse parent," and since. I have not yet found a style that fits my way of being. I know in my gut that Luna is showing me a new way that is already within me, but I have to be strong and determined enough to do it. When I work with her and pretend to be powerful and knowledgeable, she sees right through it.

I feel like I'm working entirely from intuition here, which you would think would be where my confidence is, but I haven't yet found the sweet spot of intuitive training or teaching. I will. I have found ways that align with my beliefs, but any type of "method" seems to get me off track.

I'm practicing intuitive training, which means that each horse I work with is going to do things in a different way, and is going to respond to different methods. I know this in my heart. They are all so individual, so saying, "Do this for all horses" isn't going to work. If Luna was a different horse, one I could control into doing this or that, I wouldn't be standing at this place, needing to be taught by Spirit, but alas, I have asked for this and so here I stand!

As I finish writing this, I look up from my computer and out the window. I see Luna standing, meditating in the sun, radiating her power.

I went back and stood with Luna during her dinner and allowed more understanding to filter into my awareness. This is what came to me. Luna and I are each acting in the world the way we have learned, not who we are.

I then had a conversation with my husband and kids. We discussed how important it is to reflect on who we are at the soul level. How we tend to be drawn away from who we are just by living in this society, but that it's important to remember, or at least be curious about, who we really are, and keep bringing more of that through.

The kids mentioned that it's easier for us to remember the way they were when they were little. And then we had a beautiful conversation about how they all showed themselves to the world as youngsters.

There is stress that comes with not being who we are. I call it the "vibrational bounce." The anxiety that comes from not being me has caused me years of unsureness, lack of confidence, and keeping myself small. It has caused this for many of us.

And so, moving forward with Luna, I commit to showing up with as much connection to who I am as possible, to be fully in my body when I work with her, and to focus on her soul, not on the behaviours that she is showing up with. It's so beautiful.

Suggestions from the horses for balancing and cleansing the 5th energy centre:

1. Speak your truth.
2. Listen to the Wild within you.
3. Commit to following the path of your Wild.
4. Listen intently to others, not just their words and their actions.
5. Learn animal communication.
6. Learn to listen deeply to your body.
7. Be unrelenting about being in integrity.
8. Walk your talk.
9. Show the world your gifts. Create with abandon!
10. Sing, good or bad — nobody cares, just sing! Nature wants you to sing!
11. Stretch and open the front and back of your neck energetically. So much intuitive information is coming into you from the back of your neck.

Journaling questions:

- Am I honest about who I am? Do I show up authentically?
- Do I express my feelings and my needs clearly?
- Do I interrupt others or do I speak quietly and can't be heard?
- Do I find myself saying what I think other people want to hear or am I clear and authentic in my speech?
- Do I listen to my soul self and follow its lead?
- Affirmation for 5th energy centre: I am Truth.

6th Energy Centre/ Third Eye

6th Energy Centre
Third Eye

You don't *have* a soul. You *are* a soul. You *have* a body.

The Wild in the 6th centre, located on the forehead between the eyebrows, feels like a deep knowing. It feels like expansion, beyond the mind. It knows the messages of the soul. It's deep intuition that sends us messages every day for where we are going. Our intuition helps us to feel our way forward instead of living from our heads. The work in this area is to balance intuition with intelligence. In a highly rational world, we are in continual battle between head and heart. Our heart holds our deepest knowings and when we spend more time there, our intuition opens to let the light in.

Dreams are whispers from your soul

I used to dream about Bear often. Throughout my life, Bear has been a regular visitor to my life. When I was nine, I was riding my bike to a friend's house in our small town, and I stopped at the end of their driveway because right in front of me, about six feet away, was a small bear. It was just eating and minding its own business. I turned my bike around and pedalled home faster than I ever had pedalled before!

From then on, I've had dreams about Bear. It used to be that Bear was chasing me, but as I started to do work with the horses, Bear was more often ahead of me, looking over her shoulder, encouraging me to follow her. This, to me, is an invitation from Bear, who signifies power, strength, and courage. Bear also encourages fearlessness and leadership.

Animals show up in our lives to teach us about the next stages on our journey. Sometimes they show up in front of us, and sometimes they show up in our dreams as whispers from our soul.

Focus

"When you do things from your soul, you feel a river moving within you, a joy." —RUMI

Where is your focus? The fifth energy centre is where the intellect and the ego can be loud and strong. When society teaches us to mistrust our feelings and to disengage from our soul's voice as children, the intellect and the ego take over. They work hard to "protect" us. This "protection" looks like us avoiding feeling anything at all in case we lose control.

The ego and the intellect make us believe that we are "in control" if we don't feel anything, but in truth, we are easily controllable when we are disconnected from our body, from our heart, and from our soul. We are stubborn and our society is run on fear, so it is hard for us to trust the path of the soul.

The horses teach us to trust our inner messages, our intuition. They teach us the importance of our vibration, and that if we have a low vibration, focused on lack or unworthiness, we will attract more low vibration experiences into our lives.

My mentor calls Raven the ultimate mirror, and she really is. Any time I come to Raven with ideas about what we're going to do and how it needs to go (control), I get resistance from her. Horses are resistant in places where we have resistance and/or where the person who trained that horse had resistance. When I ask Raven to play, she shows up as a free, excited, big, powerful horse. She shows up as her Wild self. When we play, I am also free. I release the need for control. I allow whatever needs to happen, happen.

This is why I know I need to play with my horse. To find connection with her, I need to find activities that we enjoy doing together. It's the same for us humans when we run into resistance. Maybe we are scared that we won't do well in something (business, for example), so we give up or don't start. I've learned that with horses and with ourselves, when we run into resistance, it's important to have low expectations, to take small bites of a task and do them with ease, while heavily rewarding ourselves along the way.

Follow your soul

It takes a lot of faith and trust to follow the soul's path. When your soul suggests that you make a dramatic change in your life, your whole body reacts and your mind struggles and strives to reconnect with the rational. In our attempt to feel safe, which the ego wants for us, we look to the rational to guide our life. But through life, those on the soul's path know that the rational path isn't working. If you aren't following your soul's path, you know it, because you're miserable. People all over the world are convincing themselves why they shouldn't say yes to their soul's path. There are so many reasons to say no to your soul's path, and we humans will work overtime trying to keep things the same.

Horses trust life and they encourage us to do the same. Raven likes to show up in people's dreams. People have called me and said, "I have to book a session to come to the farm because I've been having dreams about a black mare."

I had a dream one night. I was in the passenger seat of a car. My friend was driving, so I knew the dream was about her. We were driving down a main road in her town and we were sitting in traffic, trying to turn left. My friend was refusing to turn left (the feminine side). Raven was really impatient in front of us on the road, right in the middle of traffic. She kept turning around, waiting for my friend to turn toward the feminine, and she wouldn't. I woke up and I called my friend, telling her my understanding of the dream. She was wide eyed and surprised at how clear this was for her. She felt deeply seen by Raven. She came for a session soon after and connected on a deeper level of what messages Raven was bringing to her from her soul.

The leader is the calmest

Eckhart Tolle in his book, *The Power of Now*, talks about the indestructible essence of our Being. He says this about the human mind: "The mind is a superb instrument if used rightly. Used wrongly, however, it becomes very destructive. To put it more accurately, it is not so much that you use your mind wrongly — you usually don't use it at all. It uses you. This is disease. You believe that you are your mind. This is the delusion. The instrument has taken you over."

The horses take us on a journey to become a leader. The leader in a herd is the calmest. The other horses come to be with the leader to feel safe. We can be that for our horses. We can calm our minds enough to feel like a safe place for our horse. But calming the mind can take years of work and understanding of our own belief systems, discerning where we have repetitive or obsessive thinking based on what society has taught us. When we calm our minds, intuition rushes in.

The soul holds all of our knowing and all the knowing of the collective. It holds our purpose, which we can only know by following our soul. The horses are the soul's voice. I always tell clients, "The horses hook you up with your soul and then they show you what is standing in your way of feeling this way all the time." The things in the way can be traumas, beliefs, self-doubt, rationalization, unworthiness, and fear.

Horses don't judge

When I'm with the horses, I can feel a vibration in me that seems to bounce all over the place and I know it's not coming from them. This is my own mind and my own constant evaluation of life as good or bad. My judgement of what I am doing, of what others are doing and of what is happening around me is all too common in humans. We ALL do this. But the horses don't. If something feels off to them, they will walk away, to a more energetically clear spot. When I have this crazy vibe going on in me, the horses say, "No thanks." They usually go somewhere else and graze, which can leave me feeling rejected and not good enough . . . which is why I was so full of judgement in the first place.

Horses are non-judgemental and clear. They see everything as energy. They don't evaluate the drama or circumstance, instead they evaluate the energy. If the energy is clear and feels good, they move toward it, and if it feels unclear or off, they move away.

Thought stopping

When we have anxiety, our minds can get very focused on something and hold onto it or worry about it for days, months, or even years. *Abraham-Hicks* calls it a "thought obsession." I have called it "chronic worry." It's like this for me: when there is any quiet space in my mind, any space between thoughts, a worrisome thought rushes in and fills the space. That thought then cycles through my brain, attracting more and more similar thoughts to itself, causing a tsunami of thinking, which leads to worry, which leads to overwhelm.

Horses are interdimensional beings, as discussed in *Linda Kohanov's* book, *Riding Between the Worlds*. Linda says about the horses, "They are here to support us in finding our highest path. They may be simply being and eating grass, but the greatest work that they are doing is invisible."

Mind/Body connection

Journal entry:

My body aches. I have woken up with an intense headache three days in a row. My stomach aches and I have diarrhea . . . again. I am so tired, I can barely drag my body out of bed out to the horses. As the horses eat, I cry. I beg them for help and explain I am ready to give up.

"I'm so tired of hurting," I tell them. "I'm really finished with enduring this pain." The horses say nothing. They just keep munching happily on their hay. With a heavy heart, I drive my son to school. When I get home and my hubby goes to his office, my body and soul drag me to the bath. I light a candle, put some oils in the bath, and listen to meditation music in hopes of feeling better. I finally turn off the music and try to drop into my own meditation with my racing mind. I focus on the sound of the fan, but my mind is bouncing all over the place. I have the impulse to venture into my own heart space and hang out there. I know I've practised my venture there enough times that I can hold a steady vibration while I'm there.

I drop into my heart space, feeling the space around me, and in walks my body. I feel the vibration of my body as a late, childlike, free spirit. It is so joyful!

I can't believe it! All these years I've been blaming my body for the digestive issues and pain, but in this meditation I can't feel any of that. It doesn't seem to exist. I forgive and apologize to my body because the truth is now revealing itself.

My attention is then drawn to my mind, all that is heavy and dark. I feel the weight of fear, worry, anger, grief — all of it is there in my mind. I see cobwebs that have formed all over my mind, showing the heaviness of these feelings.

My attention is drawn to the corner of the mind where food connection lives. It's dark and heavy. I start to dust the area off and shine it up. It feels very sensitive, but happy to be free, light and shiny. And then I move to the part of the brain that's connected to my sore shoulder, and shine that area. I then clean the whole mind, careful to clean all the folds in the brain.

When my mind is shiny and bright I ask it what it needs. The message is this: "I am like a resistant teenager. I need you to take me back to the beginning, when we started believing in fear, and re-teach me how to live in joy. You need to do less and trust the universe more. We have to play together with no expectations."

My mind continues: "Ask me what I want to do and let me tell you. It might be drawing or writing or painting or laughing or playing music. Have few expectations and big allotments of time to play within. This will release my heavy resistance and allow me to feel joy again. This will allow the body to feel better."

Wow! In my meditation, I bow deeply to my mind. I honour the journey we have been on together. I watch as my mind and body join with my all-knowing soul in a heart shape. And I am the meditation.

Happy . . . with a Wild heart

Journal entry:

I was dreaming that I was sitting in a boat, being tossed by the ocean with my parents. The storm was raging around me. Then in a flash, I was in our yard, floating up. I saw our house, and as soon as I saw it, it clicked me into a lucid dream. Instantly I was white light, within my body. Like a flash, I was all light. I was healed!

Then I woke up, and out of habit, my eyes searched for what I should be worrying about now. My mind is so used to worrying that it doesn't feel settled until it finds something to worry about! Once it finds something, it might fester about it all day.

This habit of negative focus has cost me so much time and so much joy. I have changed my whole life on the outside to be a calm, settled farm life, but still I wasn't waking up happy.

The problem was in my mind; I had this lifelong habit of worry. And worry was covering up my Wildness. I couldn't show the world who I really was when my mind was constantly searching for something to worry about. To my hyper-vigilant mind, having something to focus on felt like rest, but it was far from rest.

Rest is openness. Rest is the space in the dream of white light and openness. In my dream, my focus was only on my heart, feeling the fullness of light there.

After years of clearing old trauma and breaking down old walls, now when I wake up, I am able to bask. I fall asleep feeling the softness of the sheets and the coziness of the bed and my husband's arms around me and the quietness of the night, the brightness of the moon, the rightness of my inner world . . . and I wake up doing the same thing . . . most of the time.

Dreaming into being

Lucky for me, new beginnings are my jam! It keeps me young being excited about the next new thing. I have so many things I want to learn and do that I have to put them on a list in my head. And the thing with me is, I know that if I like the thing enough to put it on my list, I will be doing it one day!

I used to draw vision boards. When my "wuzband" and I split, and I was feeling crappy and overwhelmed and like my life was not going as planned, I drew a picture of my future.

This is how I do it: I light a candle, meditate, and get myself into a nice, intuitive space. Then I draw what I call an energetic drawing. I create a space for my soul to feel like it gets to hang out and be free to express what it wants!

We get a piece of white paper and sit with it. Then I draw whatever comes through. Simply put, I draw what I deeply desire. That first time, I drew me, my two kids (Hanna was holding a wiener dog), and a new man with a little person on his shoulders. There was love radiating through this family from the page, and so much rightness and the feeling of freedom! We were all barefoot, standing in the grass. We all had big smiles on our faces.

After I met Patrick and we had our son, Kai, we bought Zen the wiener dog (this was something I straight up forced into being because I wanted him!). Then the picture was complete, so of course, I drew another one.

This time, I drew a farm. In the top right-hand corner was a two-storey home. On the left side was a hill with Hanna and I on horseback. Zen the dog was in my arms on the horse (this part hasn't happened, because let's keep it safe right?). Patrick, Brady, and Kai were all outside playing baseball together.

This has now come true! My next picture, which is doing its work right now, has our home, full of smiles and hearts, me doing healing work surrounded by three horses outside in a vortex or spiral space, me with a bestselling book and many other books, and me receiving large sums of money — oh, and a large expansion of the business! That's a lot!

There is an empty acreage near our home that I've had a vision of since we arrived here. I'll be going about my day and get flashes of things going on over there. In my drawing, I see it as a retreat centre for horses and humans, finding their Wild again together, healing together. It's a rehabilitative sanctuary for horses and humans to heal from collective and individual trauma in both species. I see the horses running wild in the centre, while the humans visit, and live with and around them. There are off-grid tiny homes to stay in, and facilities for people to come on retreat and be close to the earth.

There are 11 horses at the retreat centre, with my three who go back and forth to our property. There's a barn with retreat space upstairs and the horses below. This is also a place for the community to gather and have barn parties!

I can feel this space. I can hear the horses running past. Often, I'll be walking to the barn and my attention will be drawn to the property, to the vibration of humans connecting deeply with nature and horses. It's so beautiful. It's a bright pink energy that I hold every time I look at or think of the property.

But right now, this possibility seems very uncertain. The property isn't available. It's stuck in a court process and might not be available for many years.

But the most beautiful thing about this unfolding manifestation is that I hold the vision. I don't erase my drawing just because it doesn't seem probable. Instead, I send love to the vision whenever I think of it, and I let it stand. I don't look at my picture every day — in fact I have put it away and don't know where it is!

But this happens with all of them. I put the pictures away and sometimes I find them and I just look at them, the ones that have already manifested, and those still in process. I hold them to my heart and magnetize to them. I feel what it feels like to be standing in this vision as if it has already happened. I feel it, and feeling it draws it to me. It's my favourite kind of magic!

Suggestions from the horses for balancing and cleansing the 6th energy centre:

1. Meditate.
2. Write down your dreams.
3. If you have an anxious or obsessive mind, learn tools for managing and calming your mind.
4. Calm your nervous system and vagus nerve. Rest often.

5. Create your visions for the future. Make them clear (make a vision board, write it in a journal, or draw a picture). Be clear about what it feels like in this new vision.
6. Be discerning and have clear boundaries about where your focus is.
7. Choose thoughts that make you feel love in your heart. If you ever feel bad about a situation, you are seeing that situation differently than your inner being. Research *Abraham Hicks* for more info about this.
8. Focus on joy.
9. Experiment with vision journeys (my online course focuses on self healing through the use of vision journeys if you want to improve your skills with this).
10. Ask the horses for answers to your questions, and then be quiet and listen.
11. Learn any intuitive craft, reading cards, runes, symbols, dreams, etc and enjoy the process of diving deeper into the realms of magic.

Journaling questions:

- Do you trust your intuition?
- Do you overthink every decision? Could you practice trusting that you know what is right for you?
- Do you analyze life to the smallest detail? Could you practice trust and allow Source to show you the beauty of synchronicity over the next little while?
- Do you judge yourself and others?
- How do you receive your intuition, through visions, sounds/voices, feelings, knowings, sensations
- Affirmation for the 6th energy centre: I am Consciousness

7th Energy Centre/ Crown

7th Energy Centre
Crown

"The Divine lives inside this place . . . It is ever changing and nothing we can conceive of, it takes a great amount of courage to surrender to this great energy within, to allow the body to feel safe, the nervous system to settle and to open to something that dissolves us into a million pieces of soft love we've never met before." —SACRED_ALCHEMY

The Wild in this centre, located at the top of the head, is Divine. It feels like sparks of energy. It looks white, and it reflects everything, All That Is. Here we are, one with everything. The Wild knows everything that ever was and ever will be. The Wild here is as connected to the earth as she is to the stars. Everything here is truth.

Oneness

Horses show up in our lives as our masters. I have followed the horses to a place that has deepened my intuition incredibly.

One day, I was standing at the barn, like I do every time I feed them. I was talking to them (often I sing to them), and I said, "I just wish I could hear everything you were thinking like words in my ears, as easily as I hear another human." Well, the universe sure hears our wishes!

Soon I was taking part in experience after experience that was deepening my intuition and my ability to hear them. After this wish, I was quickly being connected with people who were mentoring me or sharing their experiences of how they got to that place, and my intuition was deepening. I learned through this experience that my doubt was the only thing covering up my hearing.

I have read tarot for years and I use my intuition every day in my healing work with people and the horses, but I hadn't used it specifically to hone my animal communication abilities.

Now, I am able to do a full session with an animal and get a lot of information about where the animal is at and what they need. Also, I am doing Soul Readings for people before they come for sessions, and the sessions are deepening greatly in their intensity and people are deepening their healings.

This is all happening for me because I am surrendering to the Divine. I am surrendering to the Wild inside me that is taking me on this ride called life. My most comfortable place of ease is like being in a river, headed downstream, with the sun on my face. This image is the exact place that I remind myself to return to when I am stuck in my mind or when I am wrapped up in doubt.

Visions

I have been pummeled by visions of me in the circle with my helpers and guides, be they animal, human, or other.

This happened for me in real time yesterday during a session with my mentor. We were here at the farm with the herd that has formed. We were discussing the call from the herd for me to really step up and become a true member of the herd, doing the work needed in more than just a physical way. They were calling to me for a deeper connection during healing sessions with people. They were calling for me to really see their gifts and to join with them as partners on a deeper level than I had been.

The animals were asking me to join the circle of nature, to hear it and understand it on a level I had only begun to feel the edges of.

This deepening of my connection takes trust and the courage to jump off another cliff. When doing this type of consciousness and energy work, I find my mind continuously looking for a place to rest, for a feeling of stability, or, "okay, this is it!" But as it goes with expansion, there is no resting place. We need to rest within the expansion.

I know that I have kept a protective cloak around myself and my gifts in hopes of appearing normal. I have realized that in order to deepen my intuitive abilities to hear and understand nature, I must be open and patient. I can't have walls of protection and a deepening of connection. Authenticity requires a truth that is not present when I have my walls up.

There is such an ancientness to this listening, this joining with nature and spirit.

I am truly humbled by the honour that I have of living and working with these magnificent beasts and Nature. We are One.

Making peace with death

Every fear we have boils down to a fear of death. Any fear, if we're really honest about it, takes us to this place. Death scares us. I was scared of my parents' death and being left alone, which is essentially being scared of dying, because being alone is synonymous with dying for a child. I turned myself inside out and made myself miserable in an attempt to avoid death. But this is the thing about death: it's only scary because it's unknown.

We don't know what it feels like to die. We don't know where we go and what we do there. We feel like it's an ending. Children ask about death often because they just don't know. And anything unknown terrifies us.

Our old horse Piper died recently. We had to make the choice with the vet to put him down, and that was the worst part. Making the choice of death for another being felt wrong. But luckily, my connection with the horses is so strong that I'm able to know when things feel right.

I had started to get the strong feeling earlier in the year that he was tired. I had a vision of him walking up to me and lying down in front of me saying, "I'm tired." I wasn't at all ready to make the decision at that time, because despite the fact that he was around 30 years old, he was still doing pretty well.

So I held this information that he was tired in my awareness, knowing that I didn't have to do anything about it right away. Just because he was tired didn't necessarily mean he was ready to go — but it opened up the conversation and started my readying process. I talked to a couple of mentors and the vet, and got the green light for Piper to carry on through the winter, but I knew, and I couldn't forget that he had shown me he was tired. I talked to him a few more times and asked him to give me a sign if he was really ready, like lying down and having a hard time getting up, or something else that was clear to me.

The day before he died, I just knew. Intuitively, something just grounded. It felt like a lightning rod that had been floating around in the air, and it finally found its ground and I just knew. I was so sure that this is what he wanted that it all happened within 24 hours of that moment.

It was December 31st, the day Piper died. He had been having a really hard time at night because he was fully night blind and anxious in the dark. He was more anxious in the day as well, and was following Raven around everywhere. She was good with him and was fine with him following right at her hip all the time.

But in the night, he would lose her and call out. His anxiety was causing the other horses, including Raven, to bully him at night. At feeding time, Piper, normally a dominant horse, first in line for his mash and chasing everyone else off, was running off into the night in fear, and sometimes the girls were kicking him because he wasn't making "herd sense" anymore. I also think he was a threat to the herd.

The vet said too that a horse that doesn't make sense to its herdmates is a danger to them. We tried everything to keep him safe, including keeping him separate from the others, but when he blew through two fences at a huge danger to himself (he got stuck in a metal fence and dragged it halfway across the field around his leg in the dark on Christmas Day), we had to make a choice. He was also starting to have trouble with his back end and was becoming unable to get up without a lot of stress.

I had entertained fantasies of just letting him have his death process, do end of life care, and be there for whatever he needed, but it didn't turn out that way, unfortunately. The day before he died, he came to me and said that was it. He was done. I told him that I could see and feel that, but that I wanted to be really sure, and asked him to send me a sign. We agreed on 11:11 because that's my sign for everything.

Sure, I see 11:11 often because I'm so attuned to it, but that day, I saw it every possible time, and in more than just the clock. The weird thing was that my family was involved in telling me too, even though they didn't know it was my agreed upon sign with Piper. My son told me it was 11:11 in the morning and then my husband told me at night after I had already seen that it was. I saw it a few more times during the day, so I had no doubt in my mind that Piper was ready.

The day it happened, we were all present except for my older son, who doesn't feel as close to the horses and wasn't comfortable with the whole thing. My youngest son wanted to be outside with us all when it happened. As a very sensitive child, I thought he might have a hard time with the realness of it (also he's been having some "fear of death" experiences at bedtime lately).

Kai was part of the whole thing, and I haven't heard anything from him about it other than joy and curiosity. But when a family member passed two days later, he had a hard time with it (even though he didn't know who it was), because it happened and he hadn't been there. Interesting how afraid we are about the unknown.

Anyway, the overwhelming fear of death that I used to have has reduced itself in direct proportion to how much my trust in life has increased. I didn't trust anything. I thought I was here to do it all, and if I couldn't do it all, we would all perish. Now I realize that I can trust life. I know that I can trust the Wild in me to show me the way, and if that is death, then so be it.

The moment Piper died, I felt him fly into our hearts. Every time I start to feel sad about the loss of his physicalness, I feel him expanding inside my heart. It's beautiful, and it's more than I could have ever asked for as confirmation that we are eternal. That our soul, our Wild, never leaves.

Messages

"Let yourself become living poetry." —RUMI

This book is about the places in life where spirit means earth. The animals are one such place and so are we. Like the animals, we stand on this earth. Our arms reach up to allow source to flow through us, and our feet touch the earth. The difference between us and the animals, though, is vast. Let's let them teach us what power we have when we reside in this place of oneness, of connection, of fierce presence.

Every day the horses send me messages. I have always been attracted to symbols. My intuition has always come in words and symbols. Every day I do either a tarot reading, or I meditate with the horses, or I go for a walk and meditate in nature to receive these messages. These are some of the messages I've received from the horses over the past while:

- Let your soul lead.
- Give up the need to control.

- Connect your heart and your head.
- They feel us and love us deeply and powerfully.
- They want us to protect them and care for them not just physically, but emotionally too.
- The herd protects its herd mates with strength and conviction.
- They are powerful and connected to spirit. So am I.
- We use our whole sensing system to hear them and to know them.
- We humans make a big hairy deal out of things that are really no big deal to the horses.
- Feel it, move your body, and go back to grazing.
- Connect deeply to the sacredness of nature.
- They love us intensely, but don't show it in the same way that humans do.

Akashic Records

A had a dream where Luna was saving me from the ocean. I was face down at the ocean's edge, and she was dragging me out by the right arm. She said to me, "I'll save you." This dream didn't make sense to me until today.

It's Winter Solstice, 2020. A big deal, here on the earth. The energies are high and ripe for moving forward past "stuck" issues and anything with old energy. Many of us have spent so many years feeling stuck or moving forward, but at a snail's pace with our issues. Today, the feeling is that the energy will be new and that we will be easily about to move up and out of the energies of these issues.

I woke up this morning and was so grateful to be able to fall back asleep. During a short dream, Luna escaped from the front gate and went across the road. I went out and looked for her, but couldn't find her. I returned to the gate and there she was, ready to head back in. This dream also didn't make sense to me until later in the day.

Our power went out today at Soulfarm, and possibly on the whole island. This isn't a rare occurrence, so we took the opportunity to play board games and read books. I was sitting beside my son on the couch and I decided to meditate on peace for the world. As I slipped easily into meditation, Luna was there, ready to have an adventure with me. Usually, when I go on a vision journey, Raven is the one who shows up and takes me on the journey. Raven has been quiet recently, though, as obviously Luna and I have work to do together.

Luna walked beside me and I felt that we were going to a deep place. I felt myself going deep inside my psyche to find old things and ancient ways. We were in the ocean together, swimming effortlessly in the deep, like mermaids. We found Blue Whale. We all went together to the ocean floor. I felt like we were diving into the Akashic Records, which are held within the energetic field. I picked up a large shell, and underneath it flowed a whole package of information for me. It was all about letting go of the old and of any dis-ease. I was asked to demand from my body that it re-adorn itself with "Full-Ease." I asked and my body obeyed. Blue Whale was holding a deep, feminine space for this work to happen. When the work was complete and my body was new, Luna and I emerged from the ocean.

For the first time in a vision or in real life, Luna asked me to get on her back. I could feel my heart and solar plexus bursting with light as I saw myself ride her across the world. As we flew over the ocean together, I saw an intense, powerful light flow throughout the entire ocean and through all of the oceans on earth.

This was an incredible experience for me to have on this day of solstice, the day of bringing back the light.

The Akashic Records, simply put, are an imprint of every potential or possibility, past, present, and future. They are potentials held within the energetic field that can be and are changed by the choices we make with our free will.

The reason I bring up the Akashic Records is this: When Luna took me deep into the ocean and we saw Blue Whale, we were looking into the Akashic Records. There was a sequence of visions that came to me over several months that started with Luna telling me in a dream that she would "save me." They culminated today in this vision where she took me to the depths of the ocean.

Whether there is more to this line of healing or not, I know that through this experience with Luna, we have changed my Akashic Records. They are changing based on every decision we make, and I know that she has been guiding me and leading me to make the decision to be fully at ease in my body. This will change my lifetimes, past, present, and future.

Circle of 13

I wrote earlier about a shamanic journey I had during my year of training on the Andean Path of the Medicine Wheel. During every shamanic journey, I ended the journey by coming to a clearing where there was a fire. Surrounding the fire was a circle of 12 beings who I knew were my supporters — some animal, some human, and some spirit. I didn't ever have names and faces for each supporter, I just felt it was a circle of support.

During my final journey on the last weekend of the year, I finished by coming to the clearing and seeing the circle of 12. This time was different, though. Instead of standing outside the circle, I was asked to join it. Together, we became the circle of 13.

This was a powerful vision for me and became a part of my being. I have a favourite pond on my forest walk where I can feel the circle of 13. As I pass the pond, I ask questions for my walk — or I just connect and give thanks to these energies. They have always felt supportive and healing.

One day, after meditating with the horses, I was listening to a channelled message. It was about something else, and then all of a sudden, they were talking about the circle of 13. I was doing dishes and did a double-take when I realized what they were talking about.

The messaging about this became clear to me. The channeling described the Circle of 13 as a healing space like no other. It's a new space that we're moving into with the new earth energies of the Aquarian Age. It's a healing space where the colour is the greenest green, and where we can look within for whatever healing we're ready for. Within this space, we can experience spontaneous healing.

After hearing this and feeling the truth of it sink into my being, I knew why I had been delivered this Circle of 13 information throughout the years. Since the beginning of Soulfarm, I have aspired to create a space of healing where people will come, and if they choose, be healed. People can come and experience a deep connection to their body and soul. They can then choose to continue with that connection, or they can choose to go back to their old ways.

The horses are offering us this new space of healing. They are hooking us up with our soul selves and allowing us to make the choice to heal. It is our choice whether we want to say yes.

Suggestions from the horses for balancing and cleansing the 7th energy centre:

1. Spend time in a headstand or looking at the world upside down.
2. Meditate with horses while connected to Spirit. Ask, "What do I need to know?"
3. Learn to channel.
4. Connect to the sacredness of All That Is.
5. Find bliss in your life and follow it every day.
6. Feel into your purpose during this life. What is your path of service?
7. Pay attention to the synchronicities in your life. What symbols show up for you?
8. Face and look at your fear of death. Make peace with death. Imagine how the animals feel about it.
9. Practice movement while connected to Spirit. Dancing, Qi Gong, walking with your heart open, anything where you feel the energy of Spirit moving through you and you are in a state of allowing.
10. Learn to trust the magic. Dive into experiences and be so present that life comes to you and moves you like never before.
11. Choose to live in a new paradigm. Choose a new birth at this time. Have a ceremony around your birth and create your new self, healed.

Journaling questions:

- What archetypes do you feel working through you in this life? Make a list, e.g. mother, teacher, goddess, alchemist, visionary, mystic, storyteller.
- Can you trust that you will be brought to your purpose if you follow the nudges within your heart? Why or why not?
- Who are you at the core of your being, after you drop all of the labels?
- What animal has come up for you repeatedly throughout your life, in dreams or in real life meetings? What message might they have for you?
- What could a spiritual practice look like for you? How could you start every day feeling grounded and connected to spirit?
- Affirmation for 7th energy centre: I am Magnificent.

For more information about energetic practices and the work we do at Soulfarm, please visit ***www.soulfarm.ca***

Red Earth

Red mud
our roots sink, feeling a connection, a place, a home.
Secure. Nothing to do.
An orange painting with vanilla scents and dances on the breeze,
hanging on a clothesline feeling with all the senses.

The sun, yellow, freshening.
All is known, all is accepted.
The self stands with warmth.
A river of green love, fireworks, opening, expansion,
encompassing, accepting, unconditional,
Sacred.

Listen to the blue sky.
Truth blows in the wind, is written on a cloud.
Dark night sings lullabies
We know, we see stars
Stars of life, of freedom, of surety.

White is a rainbow.
The wind is a rainbow.
Droplets of connection,
of life played in a raindrop other spaces part of all
Every drop, one of everything.

—THIRZA VOYSEY

Conclusion

This has been my journey of healing with the horses. The healing journey doesn't go in a straight line. Instead, it takes a winding road through experiences that show us the truth of ourselves. This journey takes us through a house of mirrors where we see things that are true and untrue about ourselves. We feel our way through, led by our hearts to connect to everything that feels like home, like light.

I have learned from the horses to stay on the path of light. If something feels dark, I will look at it and transform it. I will see where it lives in me, and go there to experience it to its fullest. Then I will walk on to what feels like light. I will stand in that light and shine all that I have and all that I am to the world.

Healing is not something that just happens on the physical or even physical/mental/emotional levels. Healing is a reconnection of you with your soul. Healing is a realignment of you with your Wild. Soulfarm is a physical space where this healing journey can happen. The first step is making a promise to yourself that you will embark. That's it. No promises to yourself to end up at a certain place at a certain time with a certain outcome, just a promise to take the first step . . . then see what kind of magic comes your way!

Epilogue

Journal entry:

The horses have come to me at a time in my life when I needed to connect to my heart and to my Feminine. They have brought me to my knees in awe as they share their unconditional love with me. They have helped me to open my heart and become the magical child again.

In my dream last night, the Feminine arose. She spoke to me through time and space. Her message to me was . . . it's time!

I feel the Feminine in me today. She moves in me, calling for quiet, for passion, for knowing. All my life, I have been unsure, confused by the power I felt within me and the contrasting messages from the world outside.

But tonight, under the full moon, I feel the intensity of my emotions. They are a river moving within me.

I felt the moon before I knew she was full. I felt her power in my womb.

I adore this feeling of my intense power. I feel my alignment and it feels unstoppable, like a train.

I want this feeling to spill over from tonight into all of my days. I want to gather it and wear it like a necklace as I walk in tomorrow's daylight. This is my wish.

I blew this wish into the Lemurian crystal that lives on my bedside table. She will hold this power for me in case I falter. She will help me remember this feeling when I want to come back to it and paint or write it. She will remember.

Every single day, four times a day, I walk to the barn. One day as I walked out of the house into the dark, I heard Raven blowing out air from her nostrils in greeting beside me. The black horse was almost invisible in the dark.

She walked away from me toward the barn and as she did, she looked over her shoulder and said, "The Wild in me sees and deeply honours the Wild in you."

Finding and connecting with our Wild will heal us.
Every. Damn. Time.

Come visit us in person at the farm or online for healing sessions, intuitive coaching, or mentorship opportunities.

Follow Thirza on **Instagram** @soulfarmsanctuary
Follow Soulfarm on **Facebook** @soulfarmhealingco
Join the Soulfarm mailing list to stay updated on new books and farm experiences at **www.soulfarm.ca**.

Acknowledgements

This book has been floating around in my head for 12 years. As I was digesting events in my life, my mind and heart would be writing about them, both physically and inside my mind. In the end, I had to write the story down because I got tired of listening to myself tell people, "I'm doing this and this and, oh ya, I'm writing a book." I wanted so badly to start saying, "I'm an author." So I sat down with all of the journals and the documents on the computer and compiled them all. Finally, this project feels complete, but my mind and heart keep writing, and I keep living, so I know there will be more books.

I can't thank my editor Carolyn Masson enough, for her efforts and long days of work on this book. Your feedback has been invaluable. Thank you to Denisa Reyes for her wonderful photographs of the horses and myself.

Thank you to everyone who has come to Soulfarm and taken part in the services we offer here, or volunteered with us in some manner. Your support of the farm has made this book possible with your investment in your own healing.

Thank you to my brilliant book and cover designer, Patrick Belanger from Drifter Media, who also happens to be my beloved. The universe was really crafty in answering my calls for a lover and a designer in the same person! You are so supportive of all my ideas and always there with your mad skills in bringing my ideas to life, better than I could have imagined (even though I know I always think I have the best ideas). Also, thank you for loving me and being patient and unendingly supportive of my creations and all the emotions we have to wade through to get them out into the world!

Thank you to my mentor, Halliday Walsh, Chiron Holistic Health Services, for holding space for me to rise into my magnificence and teaching me to do the same for others. Thank you for your constant grounded reactions to my worries about the horses and for heavily supporting my grand dreams, always inspiring me that I can make them come true!

Thank you to all of my busy bee readers for being excited to do early reads of the book and giving wonderful and useful feedback! As soon as I invited a community to surround my book, I knew that nothing could stop its explosion into the world: Gina Villares, Pat McCue, Randi Nykwist, Clara Moon Song, Tracey Diamond, Carey Marshall, Tammy McGrath, Mercedes Zetino, Chris Wood, Brooke Harris, Jenni Reusse, Carol Weaver, Jee Lam, Andrea Hounslow-Miller, Sue Murray and Denisa Reyes.

A huge bucket of carrots and apples to the horses, both matter and spirit, who have helped me with the stories and insights. Thank you from the bottom of my heart for helping me on my healing journey and for showing up every single day for me. Thank you for putting up with me as I learned your ways. Thank you for always loving me and holding me within your circle of consciousness. I am forever grateful. And thank you for teaching me the art of surrender and softening my heart with your huge hearts.

I am hugely grateful to my three children, Hanna, Brady, and Kai, for being my guiding lights for always. Thank you for inspiring me to be my best self no matter what! Without you, I'm not sure I would have had the courage to always follow my soul's path.

I would like to thank my parents for always being there for me no matter what and supporting me in my love for animals from the beginning with rabbits, dogs, cats, and guinea pigs.

Finally, thank you to my soul. Thank you for being loud and bossy and never taking no for an answer! You have led me on the most beautiful journey so far! I look forward to our continued walk through this exciting adventure called life!

About the Author

Thirza Voysey is a woman who, when she heard the words, "I don't know if I want to be married anymore," decided that she was no longer going to live a life stifled by fear. She decided in that moment to make a commitment to her soul that she would allow her soul to lead the way.

This decision changed her life in so many ways, and now she lives on a beautiful Gulf Island off the west coast of Canada, on a farm aptly named "Soulfarm." She lives with her new husband, her three children, two horses, two goats, two dogs, and one cat. Thirza is an intuitive guide who partners with horses to help humans online and in person at the farm. She also writes and paints in her barn studio, surrounded by nature.

You can find Thirza online at ***www.soulfarm.ca***

Follow Thirza on **Instagram** @soulfarmsanctuary
Follow Soulfarm on **Facebook** @soulfarmhealingco
Join the Soulfarm mailing list to stay updated on new books and farm experiences at **www.soulfarm.ca**.

Introduction
Oxford Languages — "wild" definition

Picasso, Pablo (s.d.), s.l.

Coming out of hiding
Estes, Dr. Clarissa Pinkola (1992, 1995) Women Who Run With the Wolves: Myths and Stories of the Wild Woman Archetype, United States: Ballantine Books

Soul Craving
Estes, Dr. Clarissa Pinkola (1992, 1995) Women Who Run With the Wolves: Myths and Stories of the Wild Woman Archetype, United States: Ballantine Books

Be in Harmony with Yourself
Jung, C.G. (s.d.) s.l.

Medicine Horse Farm
Abraham Hicks (s.d.) www.abrahamhicks.com, s.l.

Searching for Soulfarm
Isis, Tara (s.d.) www.wildwomansisterhood.com

Horse Magic
Sadhguru Vasudev, Jaggi (s.d.) s.l.

Being highly sensitive
Gill, Nikita (s.d.) s.l.

Kohanov, Linda (2007) Way of the Horse: Equine Archetypes for Self-Discovery, California: New World Library

Erickson, Victoria (s.d.) www.victoriaerickson.com, s.l.

The Horses Point us to our Wild
Hanh, Thich Nhat (s.d.) s.l.

1st energy centre
Isis, Tara (s.d.) www.wildwomansisterhood.com

Kroeschel Films (s.d.) Grounding, One Paw Productions, s.l.

Ober, Clint, Sinatra, Stephen T., Phd, Zucker, Martin (2010) Earthing: The Most Important Health Discovery Ever?, Basic Health Publications, Inc.

Fierce presence
Hetenyi, Dr. Mia (s.d.) www.sacredalchemyhealing.com, s.l.

Tolle, Eckhart (2000) The Power of Now: A Guide to Spiritual Enlightenment, California: New World Library

Hicks, Abraham (s.d.) s.l.

2nd energy centre
Isis, Tara (s.d.) www.wildwomansisterhood.com, s.l.

Hicks, Abraham (s.d.) s.l.

Green, John Mark (s.d.), s.l.

You are enough
Nin, Anais (s.d.), s.l.

Burning through emotion
Kohanov, Linda and McElroy, Kim (2007) The Way of the Horse: Equine Archetypes for Self-Discovery, California: New World Library

Rinpoche, Chogyam (s.d.), s.l.

Control
Tolle, Eckhart (2000) The Power of Now: A Guide to Spiritual Enlightenment, California: New World Library

Joy melts the walls around the heart

Hicks, Abraham (s.d.) www.abrahamhicks.com, s.l.

Wellbeing is our natural state
Tolle, Eckhart (2000) The Power of Now: A Guide to Spiritual Enlightenment, California: New World Library

Surrender
Isis, Tara (s.d.) www.wildwomansisterhood.com, s.l.

Nichol, Josh (s.d.) www.joshnichol.com, s.l.

Breathe
Butterflies rising (2015) www.butterfliesrising.com, s.l.

Honesty
Disraeli, Benjamin (s.d.), s.l.

Integrity
Sams, Jamie & Carson, David (1998, 1999) Medicine Cards, New York: St. Martin's Press

Fairchild, Alana (2018) Earth Warriors Oracle Guide Book, Victoria, Australia: Blue Angel Publishing

Focus
Rumi, (s.d.) s.l.

The leader is the calmest
Tolle, Eckhart (2000) The Power of Now: A Guide to Spiritual Enlightenment, California: New World Library

Thought stopping
Hicks, Abraham (s.d.) www.abrahamhicks.com, s.l.

Kohanov, Linda (2003) Riding Between the Worlds, California: New World Library

7th Energy Centre Crown
Hetenyi, Dr. Mia (s.d.) www.sacredalchemyhealing.com, s.l.

Rumi, (s.d.) s.l.

Manufactured by Amazon.ca
Bolton, ON